THESE SCHOOLS BELONG
TO YOU AND ME

THESE SCHOOLS
BELONG TO
YOU AND ME

WHY WE CAN'T AFFORD TO
ABANDON OUR PUBLIC SCHOOLS

DEBORAH MEIER

AND

EMILY GASOI

BEACON PRESS, BOSTON

BEACON PRESS
Boston, Massachusetts
www.beacon.org

Beacon Press books
are published under the auspices of
the Unitarian Universalist Association of Congregations.

20 19 18 17   8 7 6 5 4 3 2 1

This book is printed on acid-free paper that meets the uncoated paper
ANSI/NISO specifications for permanence as revised in 1992.

Text design and composition by Kim Arney

Some names have been changed to protect individuals' identities.

Library of Congress Cataloging-in-Publication Data
Names: Meier, Deborah, author. | Gasoi, Emily, author.
Title: These schools belong to you and me : why we can't afford to abandon
our public schools / Deborah Meier and Emily Gasoi.
Description: Boston : Beacon Press, 2017. | Includes bibliographical references.
Identifiers: LCCN 2017018315 (print) | LCCN 2017028713 (e-book) |
ISBN 9780807024744 (e-book) | ISBN 9780807024737 (hardback)
Subjects: LCSH: Public schools—United States. | Education—Aims and
objectives—United States. | Democracy—Study and teaching—United States.
| Democracy and education—United States. | Education and state—United
States. | BISAC: EDUCATION / Educational Policy & Reform / General. |
EDUCATION / Philosophy & Social Aspects. | EDUCATION / Essays.
Classification: LCC LA217.2 (e-book) | LCC LA217.2 .M455 2017 (print) |
DDC 371.010973—dc23
LC record available at https://lccn.loc.gov/2017018315

*To our colleagues and to the families
with whom we worked to build public schools
for a more equitable and democratic future*

CONTENTS

PREFACE

I MET DEBORAH MEIER in the summer of 1997 when I applied for a job at the Mission Hill School, which would open its doors for the first time that September. I was a young teacher in my twenties with two years of classroom experience under my belt. Deborah, on the other hand, had been in the field for over three decades. She had been directly involved in starting four internationally recognized democratic public schools and had a hand in opening scores more in New York City; she was by then in her mid-sixties, the age when most people consider retirement. But Deborah, impatient to jump back into the bustle of school life after a short reprieve, was gearing up to start yet another small, democratically governed school, this time, to my great fortune, in my then hometown of Boston.

I had read Deborah's first book, *The Power of Their Ideas*, the year before I began at MHS and I was completely taken with it. I felt as if the voice, Deborah's voice, was speaking directly to me, to my aspirations as an activist and as a novice educator. Since that time, Deborah has become my mentor, my moral north star, and my dear friend. I have grown immeasurably professionally and personally from having had the opportunity to work with her during our time at the Mission Hill School, and it has been an incredible journey and deep honor to work with her on this project.

Thus, the publication of this book in September 2017 marks twenty years since the Mission Hill School first opened its doors, as well as two decades of friendship and work together. But even as this is an auspicious year for Deborah and me as friends and colleagues, it is also a year of intense national foreboding, for public education and for democracy writ large. The 2016 election of an imperious billionaire to the presidency threatens to transform the fundamental essence of our nation, from a democracy with some autocratic tendencies to an autocracy with (if we the people are vigilant and our institutions enduring) some residual democratic tendencies. Indeed, a report from the watchdog organization Freedom House has put the United States on its "Countries to Watch in 2017" list, including us among nations that "may be approaching important turning points in their democratic trajectory."[1] Though we started writing this book before the 2016 election, we now feel an even greater sense of urgency around the need to call out thinly veiled attacks on public institutions—the pillars of our democracy—and to share our experience of what public education can be if, in Deborah's words, we take seriously the "radical—and wonderful . . . idea that every citizen is capable of the kind of intellectual competence previously attained by only a small minority."[2]

—Emily Gasoi

I OWE A VERY SPECIAL THANK-YOU to my friend and coauthor, Emily Gasoi, for making this book possible. She played a central role in the conception of how to organize the chapters so that we could tell our shared stories. The topic, democracy and education, has been a lifelong obsession (correction: actually, the democracy part has been lifelong, while the education part didn't take hold until about fifty years ago, long enough!). When we started working on the book, it was a fully joint venture. But along the way, my eyesight got worse and worse, and finally, in April of 2016, when we were really in the midst of it, my eyes more or less gave up. I now have to rely on the kindness of my electronic devices to read to me and "write" what I dictate orally. In short, much of the work finishing this project has rested in Emily's hands, which were, meanwhile, also busy with family, her five-year-old daughter, Frankie, and her other work. She deserves credit for all the book's strengths and none for its weaknesses.

—Deborah Meier

INTRODUCTION

Emily Gasoi

I MET MY FRIEND ERIN, a fifth-grade teacher in a DC public school, for dinner one evening toward the end of the school year. She had come from work and was in an uncharacteristically irritable mood. When I asked her what was wrong, she explained that a high-level administrator from the superintendent's office had visited her school that day and had spoken for thirty minutes or so about "best practices" he'd observed taking place at a well-known charter school in California. In the classrooms, he explained, he saw students engaged in projects, asking questions, discussing ideas, and excited to talk with him about what they were working on. He saw teachers popping in to observe one another's classrooms. After students left for the day, he observed teachers working together to help one of their colleagues improve an aspect of a lesson with which she was grappling.

"These are the kinds of practices," he concluded, "we need to see more of here in DC schools." Erin explained that she was overcome with a range of emotions listening to this administrator speak. At first she was filled with hope—yes, these were the kinds of practices she too knew were best, and she agreed that such a change would greatly benefit the students and teachers in her school. But then her hope faded to the more familiar feeling of frustration, as she remembered the state accountability plan recently passed by the superintendent's office in which 70 percent

1

of schools' quality would be based on student test scores, and over half of the evaluation determining whether her salary should reflect that she is a "highly effective" teacher would also be based on student test scores. The curriculum that Erin is mandated by the superintendent's office to use is 100 percent aligned with the state test. Erin was left puzzling out how to square the administrator's rousing words with the reality of her daily work within a system that allowed almost no room for her own professional or creative input.

Erin's story vividly captures the insidious cross tide of mixed messages and misguided priorities in which educators find themselves trapped. On the one hand, we are living at a time in which we know more than ever, based on scholarly research and educators' practical knowledge, about how students learn best (primarily, though not exclusively, through observation, social interaction, play, practice, and experience)[1] and about how organizations change and thrive (which, among other things, depends on the informed engagement and bolstered capacity of those who will carry out the changes, as well as the time and *trust* required for practitioners to make and learn from their mistakes).[2] But on the other hand, our current education policies—focused as they are on high-stakes, top-down mandates tied to the production of numeric data—reflect none of the best practices that only the most determined innovative schools manage to model, or that research and practitioner knowledge have borne out. In such a system, in which practitioners do not have the right to exercise their own professional judgment, it is hard to imagine how they will model for children—the future stewards of our *commonweal*—what it means to be empowered citizens in a society that is predicated on the lofty premise of being governed of, for, and by the people.

We write this book about our experience working in democratic schools and in the wider arena of education reform in part to illustrate what we mean when we say "these schools belong to you and me." But we also do so because the kinds of schools that we describe throughout these chapters—schools that have pioneered and that have attempted to sustain their innovative, democratic, or just demonstrably *good* practices—are in danger of disappearing. Indeed, it is not an overstatement to say that, in 2017, our very institution of free, universal education is at risk of succumbing to the forces of free-market ideology, which have overtaken our national sensibilities.

Over the last twenty-five years, entire public school systems in urban and rural communities across the country—from the City of Brotherly Love to the Motor City, from the Windy City to the city surrounded by Gulf Stream waters—seem to be sinking into the quicksand of lost causes or fighting their way back from the shock therapy of wholesale privatization.

In many cases, public schools, both in-system and charter, are threatened or closed because they are labeled failing based on student test scores. Public schools in every state have been deemed "economically unsustainable" due to dwindling enrollment and draconian budget cuts. In Secretary of Education Betsy DeVos's home state of Michigan, as in others, entire school districts are losing the battle against unregulated privatization through for-profit charter management entities and voucher programs.[3] And DeVos is now poised to make Michigan a model for the rest of the country.

Against this backdrop of intense peril for our system of public education, we attempt throughout this book to tread a fine line between supporting public education while advocating for fundamental change to what education scholars David Tyack and William Tobin call the traditional "grammar of schooling."[4] Though we unequivocally support public education, elaborating at length on the problems with current attempts at dissolving our public system in favor of a free-market vision of education, we also agree with social scientists who have written for decades about how schools, in their traditional form, perpetuate existing social inequities.[5] Drawing on our own experiences as both students and educators in a variety of settings, including traditional, progressive, and "disruptive" schools (i.e., schools that disrupt the dominant social order), we attempt throughout these pages to illustrate changes to the current public school model that strengthen rather than tear down our system of universal education—an institution vital to our movement toward a more evolved democracy.

Though not always explicitly addressed in the pages of this book, we see racism as a major force in keeping schools, and our society more broadly, from truly becoming both more democratic and, not incidentally, more productive and safe. As Americans, we have never fully embraced democracy and all that it entails. Even during the first half of the last century, when soaring rhetoric about democracy as a conceptual cradle for high ideals such as freedom of movement, expression, and association was more prevalent, we have never been willing to extend such freedoms to all of our citizens. As Harlem Renaissance writer and journalist Zora Neale Hurston wrote in her biting 1945 essay "Crazy for This Democracy,"

> I accept this idea of Democracy. . . . It must be a good thing if everybody praises it like that. If our government has been willing to go to war and to sacrifice billions of dollars and millions of men for the idea, I think that I ought to give the thing a trial. . . . The only thing that keeps me from pitching headlong into the thing is the presence of numerous Jim Crow laws on the statute books of the nation. I am crazy about the idea of this Democracy. I want to see how it feels . . . [but] the Hurstons (as with most if not all Black families) have already been waiting eighty years for that.[6]

More than seventy years after Hurston wrote these words, the effects of racism still prevent us from actualizing both the more lofty and the practical aspects of our democracy—which causes overwhelming suffering for some, but hurts us all.

Minorities in this country have been systematically barred from feeling a sense of ownership, as if they have not contributed to the culture. Schools have historically perpetuated racist, ethnic, and classist societal norms by reinforcing the notion that the cultural norms and practices students bring from home are somehow deficient, a mark of inferior intelligence. This includes the commonly held belief that poor children (particularly if they are African American) lack something called "grit" or that they are language deficient. It flies in the face of the facts and is truly an "alternative" truth, in the sense that the Donald Trump administration has used the term. Black labor, blood, and sweat have built this nation, cultivated its land, harvested it bounty, and contributed inestimably to our distinctly American arts and culture; people across the globe are influenced by and attempt to imitate African American music, style, even language—and yet we claim that Black children are somehow linguistically and culturally deprived. African Americans have survived, and many have thrived, despite centuries of lawfully sanctioned oppression, and we say that they lack "grit" and the character traits of their productive white "counterparts."

Ultimately, our commitment (or acquiescence, as the case may be) to white supremacy has hobbled our society as surely as if we had amputated one of our own two legs. And for what? How can we begin to think of ourselves as a democratic nation as long as a significant (and growing!) segment of our population is made to feel that, unless they adopt dominant cultural norms, they have nothing of value to contribute and therefore no stake in a shared vision of the future? We need to face and explore not only the injustice of racism and the price we all pay for it but also its origins— what do we fear would happen if we were to live up to our most soaring national rhetoric?

Finally, a word about the title of this book, which plays on the 1940 Woody Guthrie song "This Land Is Your Land." The song is often referred to as our alternate national anthem (not to be confused with an "alt" anthem), one that is lofty and sweeping in its declaration of a shared claim to our nation's great bounty without turning away from the less lovely realities that have greatly hindered our progress toward fulfilling our democratic promise.

In one of Guthrie's more critical verses (one not often sung by schoolchildren, unfortunately), he thumbs his nose at the notion that our country might be carved up and claimed for private purposes, a theme that resonates with us in the context of saving public education from privatizing forces.

There is also an apt story about activist and musician Pete Seeger, who made Guthrie's song a regular part of his concert playlists. After one concert at which he'd sung the song, a Lakota Sioux chief, Henry Crow Dog, reportedly pointed out to Seeger the problematic claim this alternate anthem makes when considered within the context of the violent wresting of the continent from Native peoples. After this interaction, Seeger, as has been the tradition with others who have performed the song, added a verse and tinkered with the wording of the chorus. In his new version, he sang a verse from a Native American perspective and changed the last line to "this land was stole by you from me."[7]

In a sense, Guthrie's song (which, in true form for one who disdains ownership, he never copyrighted) has become a conversation, one that expands and is reshaped through human discourse. It is the kind of conversation that captures the spirit of Walt Whitman's conception of democracy when he wrote, "Democracy is only of use there that it may pass on and come to its flower and fruit in manners, in the highest forms of interaction between men [and women], and their beliefs—in religion, literature, colleges, and schools—democracy in all public and private life."[8]

In other words, democracy, if it is to endure, must be seen as much more than the vote each adult citizen casts for a representative. Neither can it remain an abstraction, but rather, democracy lives in our daily practices and interactions with others. It is in this vein that we thought about the organization of this book, writing the chapters in alternating voices: in chapter 1, Deborah gives a broad overview of how her experience in schools has shaped her vision of education for democracy and concludes with the question, *how can we hope to educate for democracy if children and the adults in their lives never have the opportunity to observe or practice it?*; in chapter 2, I draw on my own experience in schools, as both student and teacher, to reflect upon that question and to illustrate how some of the ideas Deborah shares in her chapter manifested as we worked together to start a new democratic school. I end chapter 2 with a query that Deborah's narrative addresses in chapter 3, and so on.

This way of organizing the book worked as a practical device, a way to exchange ideas based on our respective experiences working in democratically governed schools, and to offer readers an intergenerational analysis of those experiences within the context of the last several decades of education reform. But we also decided that the book should take this form based on our shared investment in dialogue as the essential animating force within a democracy. For without the ongoing exchange of ideas, the imperative to understand and empathize with another, to find common ground and compromise, democracy becomes an inert and rigid precept.

Having had the opportunity to work in self-governed schools, we have each experienced the alchemy involved in creating a shared community, evolving and cohering around thousands of conversations among and between the school's constituents. We hope that readers will find in these chapters, woven together from our individual ideas, experience, and research, a cohesive narrative addressing the role that public schools can and must play in a healthy democracy.

CHAPTER 1

THE PROBLEM AND PROMISE OF PUBLIC EDUCATION

WHAT'S WORTH FIGHTING FOR?

Deborah Meier

> We have taken democracy for granted. We have forgotten that it has to be enacted anew in every generation, in every year and day, in the living relations of person to person in all social forms and institutions.
>
> —JOHN DEWEY, 1937[1]

I HAVE BEEN AT WORK and play within the field of education for over half a century. I began as a substitute teacher in 1963 and, though I was tentative about succumbing to what was widely disparaged at that time as "women's work," it wasn't long before I was dedicating most of my waking hours to what has since become my life's work. From my first experience subbing in Chicago's notorious South Side public schools until 2004, with a few breaks here and there to try my hand at spreading some of my ideas, I worked in schools as a teacher, a union rep, a cofounder, and a principal, and was involved in schools as an activist, a parent, and a school board member. When I retired in 2004 from my position as principal of Mission Hill School in Boston, I had to adjust to a new reality—one in which my calendar became dotted with publication deadlines and speaking engagements instead of school days in the company of teachers, parents, and children.

I now spend most of my professional energy outside the stimulating bustle of school life, straddling the extremes of sitting alone writing and speaking to large groups of adults about education and democracy. As any educator will tell you, however, once you've worked in schools, almost everything you see and do relates back in some way to the formidable puzzle that is teaching. For example, a while back I had a revelation about how giving speeches to a room full of seemingly attentive and presumably well-educated adults is much like the classroom game of telephone; that is, even when my speech receives loud applause, it is not proof that the message I *thought* I had conveyed is the one that was heard—and isn't this also the case when we communicate with children in the classroom?

This suspicion of mine was validated some years ago when, after giving a well-received speech, a member of the audience came up to tell me that I had changed her life. "I'll never again worry about what kind of shoes I have to wear on public occasions," she said. Indeed, I was wearing comfortable sneakers along with my fancy speech-making dress. It was a startling acknowledgment of an unexpected sphere of influence. In many ways the example of my sneakers had an impact as great as any I have had on a single member of an audience, given how much many of us have suffered from wearing the wrong shoes. Never underestimate those unintended ways in which one influences! As such, the "education of the shoes" is not a bad metaphor for teaching itself. Since we so rarely ask ourselves what purpose the relentlessly long years of education are intended to serve, almost any impact of consequence is welcome.

When I began teaching kindergarten I grew curious to know why kids thought they came to school each day. I wondered why they imagined their parents brought them here to be with another adult all day long. I noticed that when parents came to collect their children at the end of the school day, often the first words out of their mouths were these: "Were you good today?"

Given the emphasis parents seemed to place on behavior, it was not surprising that the kids readily answered my question about why they were in kindergarten with the following assorted answers: "To learn to raise your hand," "to take your turn," "to line up," "to be quiet when the teacher is talking." In short, to be well behaved. Hardly the most exciting reasons for coming to school, but a reasonable deduction based on what the adults in their lives, including us teachers, signaled in our conversations with children and their families. Fortunately, a few children finally chimed in with "reading." My heart leapt with enthusiasm.

"And why is it important to learn to read?" I asked.

"So you won't get left back at the end of the year," virtually all answered.

"And once you do get promoted, can you stop reading?" I pushed on.

"No, because if you get to first grade, then comes second"—and on and on they went, through high school and, for some, beyond. The children, at that young age, were already aware that one needed to read in order to do well in school.

"So," I continued, "when you finally get out of school, can you stop reading at last?" They mostly responded, "Yes," but one child persisted with uncanny foresight.

"No," she said, "because if you get married and have a child, you'd need to read to him so he wouldn't get held back!"

Regardless of the content of the lessons we intend to teach, these superficial "school moves"—the "grammar of schooling"[2]—appear to be the dominant messages that many children internalize about the purpose of their twelve years of education. And unlike the audience member who approached me to share her insight about my sneakers, most children will not volunteer their thoughts on the implicit "wisdom" they are deriving from their time in the classroom. But suppose children did ask the adults responsible for making their schools what they are—"Why are we here?" Do we adults—parents, educators, superintendents, policymakers, and reformers—have a more substantive and compelling vision to impart to them?

The truth is, we do not have a strong tradition in our education system of thinking about either individual proclivities or the common good. School-improvement rhetoric, as of late, generally broadcasts misguided, unattainable claims that have little intrinsic interest to children. Consider, for example, that the most commonly repeated reform promises of the past three decades have focused on increasing accountability, raising test scores, and closing test-score achievement gaps as a proxy for preparing children for college and the twenty-first-century workforce. There has been precious little in this rhetoric that hints at the role schools might play in helping the young to find, in education reformer John Dewey's words, their "true business in life."[3]

The names of our most recent federal reform initiatives have been disappointingly devoid of vision: *Race to the Top* evokes a fast-paced contest in which children must hurry to the peak of a metaphorical summit, turning education into a zero-sum game in which there is only so much room at the top; and now, the Every Student Succeeds Act, which some hoped would signal the end to the era of No Child Left Behind, makes a particularly ludicrous claim given our system that measures success according to a test-based bell curve or rank order, ensuring that a percentage of our children will always make up the losing end of that arc.

For the most part, the notion of the "common good"—making sure all children have access to a meaningful education that helps them to develop into well-rounded citizens who have a stake in and something to contribute to the wider community—has been boiled down to getting children of color from low-income households to score as well as their more privileged white peers on standardized tests. Indeed, closing this test-score gap has been called by some the most pressing civil rights issue of our time. Ironically, the national obsession with test scores was originally justified as a way to democratize education by providing an easily understood translation of what many considered to be educational gobbledy-gook: Use a standardized instrument so all children are "fairly" assessed according to a set bar. Avoid the historic biases of teachers and the public. Offer concrete evidence instead of fancy abstract words. In short, replace supposedly subjective human judgment with presumably objective numbers.

All of this sounds reasonable enough. The problem is that, after nearly two decades on this course, it has become clear that we've actually achieved just the opposite. In the name of equity, we're using a measure based on an even more biased abstraction that virtually no one truly understands. Test data, for example, cannot shed light on ways that individuals may have been personally enriched during the time spent in school, nor have they been shown to reliably indicate preparedness for college, work, self-fulfillment, or the life of an engaged citizen. Perhaps most problematic of all is that we have become accustomed to the use of numeric data in place of human judgment in matters as important as our children's intellectual growth.

I have done extensive research on standardized testing over the decades and will address the topic further in chapter 5. But suffice to say that we do have concrete evidence that the culture of high-stakes accountability has hurt the very population it is purported to serve. The curriculum has become absurdly narrow, cutting out untested material and subjects, and schools are more segregated than ever (especially by class), as families with means generally steer their children clear of discipline-oriented, test-obsessed settings that characterize many schools serving primarily poor students, and especially poor students of color.

And while our newly appointed secretary of education, Betsy DeVos, and her supporters advocate for vouchers as a way to extend to low-income families the kinds of choices that the wealthy have always exercised on behalf of their own children, the data on charter school choice indicates that we can expect vouchers to increase, not diminish, the proliferation of separate and unequal schooling. Charter schools, with their broad enrollment policies, once held great potential to disrupt the de facto segregation that becomes entrenched in schools located in segregated neighborhoods. But the devil is in the details of how they are designed and regulated. Charters, serving only 5 percent of the overall public school population, are far more segregated by race, ethnicity, and class than district public schools.[4]

These policies not only lead us down the wrong path in terms of creating schools that children might actually want to attend, but they also contribute to a culture that discourages educators from questioning why we often find ourselves cajoling or coercing children into participating in nonsensical school routines such as working alone in silence at one's desk when few adult jobs actually require such behavior, or spending a good portion of the day or week on prepping for standardized tests that have little to do with anything of relevance in the real world.

In my experience, both as a parent and teacher, I have been struck by how strong children's voices are and how long their attention spans are when they are deeply immersed in their own play.[5] It occurred to me early in my teaching career how strange it was that the culture in most schools works to silence these playground intellectuals who come to be educated throughout their most formative and intellectually vibrant years. I began to wonder what could be so important that it would justify our essentially incarcerating kids for over twelve years of their lives?

These blunt words may seem surprising coming from a lifelong educator, but I assert that schooling, as it exists in most traditional settings, is fundamentally the legally enforced removal of children's personal liberty for five to six hours a day, 185 days each year. Why has the enduring classroom norm been to keep lively, vital youngsters sitting still at desks for twelve to fifteen years no matter what their interests and inclinations? Most inexplicably, why have so many of the most popular charter franchises designed specifically to serve poor and minority students, such as Success

Academy, the Knowledge Is Power Program (KIPP), and their emulators, used their autonomy to intensify a prison-like, zero-tolerance culture within their schools?

And, given how counter many schools run to the human drive to learn through experience, apprenticeship, and practice, we must ask how realistic it is to imagine that most children would, with enthusiasm and eagerness, voluntarily enlist in the task of being schooled. Most importantly, what exactly is it that we hope to "pass on," from one generation to the next, that justifies such a dramatic infringement on children's basic rights? What follows are elaborations on some priorities that have emerged over the last several decades, ones that my colleagues and I have grappled with to ensure that school makes sense for those closest to the action—students, teachers, and their families.

CULTIVATING THINKERS AND DECISION MAKERS

Despite my opposition to imprisoning children in institutions that make little sense to them, there are, of course, good reasons for instituting free, compulsory schooling. All societies educate a ruling class to be able to make important decisions not just for their individual self-interests but ostensibly in the interest of the larger society over which they rule. When all citizens are members of the ruling class, then all citizens need to be educated to meet their own self-interests and the interests of society as a whole. Of course, throughout history, few democracies have extended citizenship to all their inhabitants, and the United States is no exception. At the signing of the Declaration of Independence, only propertied, white men were able to vote. Everyone else has had to fight mightily to expand the circle of citizenship through enfranchisement. The struggle for voting rights continues to this day, though we now live under the pretense that all Americans are full citizens, and so all children, regardless of gender, race, or class need to be educated to make important decisions for themselves and the commonweal.

In the schools I started with colleagues in New York City and Boston, we prioritized scheduling time for teachers to collaborate and to be involved in much of the important decision making that usually falls to administrators alone.[6] We intentionally designed the physical space so that teachers would meet to discuss their daily practice within view and earshot of students, so that children would come to see their teachers as empowered adults who were committed to and versed in democratic practices. Many schools these days do create structures to facilitate at least grade-level meetings among teaching teams. The level of true collaboration that takes place or power that teachers have in these teams varies widely depending on the school organization and culture. But even in schools where teachers are fairly empowered, it is rare indeed that students are ever made aware of the kinds of ongoing conversations, planning, and grappling in which their teachers engage. And it is even less likely in most schools that students themselves will be invited to add their own ideas to decision-making processes, even when those decisions directly impact their school experience.

Building in time for colleagues to talk and think, as well as time for students and others in the community to contribute, is a critical factor in the creation of democratic schools. If you want to know whether a school is a proving ground for democracy, look at who within its walls has the time to think about the school as a whole and who has the power to weigh in on matters both critical and small. My litmus test always considers the effect a school's organization has on its various constituents' sense of power and respect. Do all constituents think they have a say in the life of the school?

Some schools carefully nurture a culture predicated on an agreed-upon philosophy and vision; others are less deliberate about the kind of culture that takes root. But one thing is certain: every school culture projects vital messages about power and status and the connection of both to decision making. While there are certainly challenges associated with democratic governance, creating a sense of collective ownership supports a vision of schools in which constituents learn the art of living together, in which we are compelled to defend the idea of a public, not private, investment in all of our children. And it is in such settings in which our young, through daily observation and apprenticeship, receive a "ruling class" education.

I know firsthand what a ruling-class education looks and feels like. When I was eight years old, my family moved from the mostly rural Larchmont, New York, to a spacious apartment on Manhattan's Upper West Side, and I began attending a progressive private school called Ethical Culture Fieldston School (ECFS). German-born educator and social reformer Felix Adler founded the school in 1878 as the "Workingman's School" to provide poor, mostly immigrant children living on the Lower East Side of Manhattan with a rich, experiential environment in the service of educating students for "good citizenship."[7] As Adler explained in the original mission statement, "We wish to send out men and women who will glory in their citizenship and be an honor to the city and the nation. We wish to make our students servants of humanity."

I thrived in this environment where we were expected to formulate our own opinions, ideas, and solutions related to the sociopolitical and scientific issues swirling around us, and where teachers and students were expected to collaborate and contribute to both upholding and influencing the evolution of the school's values. By the time I was in high school, however, it became clear to me that the school's original vision of providing a rich education for working-class children had been lost. When I looked around at my classmates, I only saw kids like me—almost all white and from families with comfortable means. As a private school, ECFS has been able to remain rooted in its progressive pedagogy and values. But as with most progressive private schools and models that were originally intended to serve the working classes, it has not managed to remain true to that founding vision.[8]

In 1963, when I started subbing in public schools on Chicago's South Side, I was deeply shaken by the many ways in which the schools undermined the most basic premises of democracy. Although it probably wasn't as bad as it was before teachers unionized, I had never in my life been treated as shabbily, as disrespectfully as I was as both a parent and a teacher in our public schools. Why couldn't schools for all children look and feel like the school I had attended? I often heard from all political sides that progressive education is for children who can "afford it," not just financially but in terms of something called "preparedness."

As we would come to understand, preparedness involves (as college readiness often does today) feeding poor minority students a stripped-down curriculum of rote facts, basic skills, and middle-class social norms that richer peers are assumed to pick up naturally. Somehow, the kind of sophisticated, experiential education that children who attend progressive private schools experienced was considered risky for poor minority children. One has to wonder if it is not considered risky by some (namely, the privileged elite) to educate everyone to feel entitled to a seat at the table and a say in what is "served."

After subbing for a year, I began to teach part-time in a series of early-childhood classrooms, first in a small school called Shoesmith in Chicago, then in the first Head Start program in Philadelphia, and finally in a half-day kindergarten in PS 144, located in Central Harlem in New York City. By the time I got to PS 144, I began to notice a pattern in the behavior of the children I was teaching. In each setting I found that the children started out timid and reluctant to talk, seeming to affirm common beliefs about what is—to this day—assumed to be indicative of poor, minority children's academic unpreparedness and their general intellectual and cultural deficits. After a few weeks, however, having set up a safe and stimulating environment, I found that children were interested in exploring everything in the room—from the sand table to the book corner, the paint, and the clay, as well as the colored pencils, the big old typewriter I picked up second hand, and the gerbils we adopted.

I worked with an assistant teacher who lived in the neighborhood where the school was located and between us we called students' parents to encourage them to visit the classroom. I began the practice—which I continued for the next forty-plus years—of writing a weekly Friday letter for children to take home to their families. And once we had support from families, and the children had made the room and the materials their own, the students' voices began to ring out in the classroom as they did on the playground, full of theories and questions and stories that connected their experience to the work and play we did together on a daily basis. My teaching experience thoroughly debunked for me the notion that children from poor families are somehow less prepared to learn or that progressive education is only appropriate for their wealthy peers.

For instance, when five-year-old Darrell insisted that his rock was "alive," I was dumbfounded. I had dutifully applied the lesson plan in the Board of Education curriculum guide. We spent Day 1 discussing living and non-living things, and on Day 2, each child was asked to bring an object to school. Darrell was the first student I called upon. I asked him to place his rock in either the box labeled "Living" or the box labeled "Non-living." He chose the "Living" box. I tried not to be discouraging while subtly attempting to correct his mistake, but he was adamant. Within twenty minutes he had converted the class by explaining that rocks can grow to be as big as a mountain and can form groups, with bigger (parent) and smaller (children) members of the same rock family.

As I looked at the next child, who had a recently plucked leaf in her hand, I decided the time had come to move on to other things. Was that leaf living or non-living? I needed time to think about where to go next with what the day before had seemed to me a simple and obvious idea. What I discovered instead was that these five-year-olds were theorizing on the cutting-edge of science. So we kept at it, arguing and looking for evidence to prove our assertions regarding the attributes of living and non-living things, on and off for the entire year. We never entirely settled that argument. But the children had formulated opinions on this and myriad other topics, and they had become versed at providing evidence to support their ideas. As a teacher, I learned to value the process children go through to make meaning, even if that required putting off the satisfaction that comes with guiding them to find the "right" answers. But, as with my five-year-olds, I probably learned most from my mistakes.

For example, a year later I pursued another grand plan for a curriculum on the importance of sunlight for living things. The children planted seeds in a dozen little containers, and once they began to sprout, we placed half on the windowsill and half in the closet for the weekend. Of course, I could have wasted less time and just told them that sun was needed for the plants to grow, but being a "good" teacher, I wanted them to discover this fact for themselves. Unfortunately, the experiment didn't go as I had expected. On Monday I came in early only to discover that the plants on the windowsill were dead, and the ones in the closet were doing just fine.

My plan for the day was thrown into confusion and, in a moment of early morning panic, I threw them all away! Despite my growing understanding of how to teach through inquiry, like many educators, I unconsciously still viewed science "experiments" as simply a vivid means for helping children to learn and memorize known scientific concepts. The notion of experiments as a means, not an end, had gotten lost. My nerve failed me exactly at the moment that real science might have entered the children's school life. The possibility of arousing their passion, their curiosity was part of my educational belief system, but it was not yet a consistent habit.

Some years later, after starting the Central Park East Schools, thirteen-year-old Frances and I happened to be studying a big old-fashioned world map on the wall, the kind that divides Asia from Europe. She turned to me and asked in a genuinely puzzled voice: "How come the East Indies are in the West and the West Indies are in the East?" I brought this amazing fact to the attention of my other students and it immediately became part of the curriculum: the history of maps, decisions made about how to represent a round earth on a flat surface, and so forth. For Frances, this experience provided practice for being part of the "deciding class." She had introduced a weighty and important subject—who made history?—by her own observant curiosity. Her question had sparked the interest of her peers, and together we explored this important topic.

We need to allow a diversity of ideas to flourish, even—or especially—those ideas that strike us as "wrong-headed," because human beings are often wrong. And as much as the current culture of accountability disallows this fact, venturing, wondering, discovering we are wrong (or not as right as we had assumed) and then allowing curiosity and perseverance to urge us on to venture and wonder some more, are at the heart of meaningful teaching and learning. We need an empowered constituency, unafraid of bringing a diversity of perspectives, including those ideas that seem unconventional, even unlikely, to the table. These kinds of exchanges are what animate the concept of democratic apprenticeship. Inviting students to put their ideas into the pot, to take a stand, to voice their questions, opinions, skepticism, and critique is what we mean when we refer to a "ruling class" education.

MAKING ROOM FOR RESISTANCE AND SHARED RESPONSIBILITY

Most Americans are familiar with the first few lines of the Declaration of Independence:

> We hold these truths to be self-evident, that all men are created equal, that they are endowed by their Creator with certain unalienable Rights, that among these are Life, Liberty, and the pursuit of Happiness. That to secure these rights, Governments . . . [derive] their just powers from the consent of the governed,—*that whenever any Form of Government becomes destructive of these ends, it is the Right of the People to alter or to abolish it.* [Emphasis added]

While these inspiring opening words remind us of the rights we are all entitled to, it is the following line, far less familiar to most, that articulates the conditions of such entitlement, admonishing that "Prudence, indeed, will dictate that Government long established *should not be changed for light and transient causes*; and accordingly all experience have shewn that mankind are more disposed to suffer, while evils are sufferable, than to right themselves by abolishing the forms to which they are accustomed" (emphasis added).

It is in this seldom-quoted line that the dilemma of democracy is defined, for it is rarely clear what constitutes a *light and transient cause* or when we can rightly say that our suffering at the hands of our government (or under local police precinct practices, untenable work-place policies, initiatives put forward by the state superintendent of schools, and so forth) has become insufferable. It is in schools where children and adults should have the opportunity to grapple with a range of hypothetical and real-world problems of varying weight and significance.

An example from Central Park East Secondary School (CPESS) offers an illustration of one way such grappling plays out. Early in the life of the school, staff introduced what they initially assumed were fairly standard, uncontested school rules: no wearing hats and no gum chewing. As it turned out, however, students pushed back against that assumption and successfully convinced enough staff that these two rules actually ran counter to other, more deeply held school values. It began with student internships.

Once a week, all CPESS students spent their school day off campus, working in a local business or community organization. In many of these settings, students noticed that the adults often wore hats (sometimes as part of their uniform, as was the case in many settings that prepared food or required protective gear) and that they often chewed gum without any ill impact on their work. Bringing these observations up in a staff meeting, students argued that our ban on hats and gum chewing contradicted our school's commitment to blurring the line between the world within and beyond the school walls. Of course, there were some work settings where these rules were also in place, but when staff were not able to make a strong case for why hats and gum were problematic in the school, we decided to modify the rules.[9]

Students were able to push back against rules they found illogical through the multiple forums for meeting that we had established when we founded the school. These forums included daily student advisories during which mixed-age cohorts (for example, seventh-eighth grades) met with their advisory teacher to discuss issues—big and small, school related and personal—that mattered to them. Staff and the parent council met regularly, but their meetings were open to the entire school community, which meant anyone could participate in, add to, or propose to change the agenda. Creating connections between the school and the community, as well as reserving a place at the table for the entire school community when it came to decision making, has proven especially essential when addressing issues that involved external challenges, some that potentially threatened the school's very existence.

For example, in 1998 the Commonwealth of Massachusetts mandated that schools use curriculum based on prescriptive state standards and administer high-stakes testing in grades three through eight. Mission Hill School staff felt strongly that both the state standards and the standardized testing were antithetical to our way of teaching and assessing. In order to address this problem, we pulled together the entire school community—staff, students, families, and board members—and collectively devised a public response and a plan for resisting the state mandate in a way that felt acceptable for all involved (more on this topic in chapter 4).

Over the years I have learned that sustaining a democratic culture depends on building practices that enable us all to develop strong habits of heart and mind through frequent *association* with one another. Something as seemingly simple as setting time aside to voice our opinions, to hear one another out, to wrestle with ideas and face dilemmas together is actually imperative. One reason this is so important is because, when under pressure (which is often, in school settings), we humans are likely to drop our democratic ideals in favor of "doing what we have to do." Adversity may bring out the best in some, but history has taught us that the habits of democracy are often the very ones we abandon under stress.

From German citizens in 1932 responding to a legacy of humiliation and economic sanctions following WWI to economically stressed British citizens living in culturally isolated communities responding to an unprecedented influx of refugees in 2016, marginalized populations that have not been educated to think critically and who have not had to consider the lives of others (as do people of color living in majority white societies) are historically more likely to vote for autocratic leaders and isolationist policies, often against their own interests.

This forsaking of democratic ideals has played out to some extent in our own country, with the election, in 2016, of an autocratic president who won the vote of many of the most economically stressed and socially isolated among us.[10] Even as President Trump dispensed with democratic habits and norms most Americans had long taken for granted, he played on enough voters' fear, frustration, and resentment and provided them with easy targets at which to direct their anger—immigrants, refugees, and, of course, ironically, an overreaching government—to win the electoral college if not the popular vote.[11] Former congressional speechwriter Rob Goodman points out what Trump's frequent political transgressions say more broadly about the state of our democratic norms: "You don't do those things, until, one day, you do. The only thing holding you back in most cases is the force of custom, and there are times and places . . . when custom is so weak that it's no force at all."[12] When we take our democratic values and practices for granted, when we do not take the time to make and remake them, then we are likely to let them slide when the going gets rough.

All of this raises a fundamental dilemma inherent in democracy, which is that it is possible to democratically elect an autocratic leader whose policies threaten the very democratic institutions that brought them to power (democratically elected presidents Recep Tayyip Erdogan of Turkey and Nicholás Maduro of Venezuela, for example, are both moving to claim vast powers in their respective countries). This dilemma only highlights the importance of revisiting the underlying purpose of having a system of free, universal education in a democracy: that is, we need a means of ensuring that we educate all future citizens, not only to be well versed in the three *R*s, and other traditional school subjects, but also to be able to see from multiple perspectives and to be intellectually curious and incisive enough to see through and resist the lure of con artists and autocrats, whether in the voting booth, the marketplace, or in their social dealings. As the 2016 election should make clear, we cannot afford to reserve such critical education for the privileged classes.

Indeed, schools must become the proving grounds for democracy, the arena where children and adults alike engage in democratic *practice* (in the daily-routine sense of the word). For what does it say about our values when those within a community—whether it be a school, a constituency, or a nation—demonstrate such a loose hold on democratic practices? In schools, what do kids learn about their rights and responsibilities as community members when we leave them to make, at best, the most trivial decisions that we ourselves care little about? And what does it say about the state of our democracy when, for example, the state government steps in and essentially tells a school community—principals, teachers, parents—that they cannot be trusted to make any but the most trivial decisions about their schools?

One reason that this seemingly self-evident proposition—that citizens in a democracy must be educated such that they develop democratic dispositions and inclinations—has proven so elusive in schools is that such dispositions often involve some degree of questioning one another's ideas, argumentation, and, in some cases, even resistance. By *resistance*, I am referring to a stance in which it's understood that one has the right to resist demands—whether they come from within or outside of the school—that will impinge upon one's personal or professional integrity or that of others in your community.

Early in my teaching career, my colleagues taught me the art of "creative noncompliance" (more on this topic in chapter 3), a form of resistance that involved deflection and, yes, a level of dishonesty in which I always regretted having to engage. But I argue that teaching without exercising judgment is not truly teaching (I have heard that the average teacher makes over a thousand decisions in a single day), and it is impossible to exercise sound, responsive judgment while also, for example, obediently following a canned curriculum, a mandated pacing guide, or a prescribed mode of instruction. And so, as most teachers and principals know, we do what we have to do to maintain integrity, for our own and for our students' sake.

Sometimes these deflections are swift and fairly harmless: a quick switch of lessons when an administrator from central office showed up unannounced, a disingenuous claim of ignorance of district regulations and an insincere promise to correct the "mistake," and the like. But sometimes educators are forced into truly compromising situations, such as being mandated to continually get students to improve their test scores from year to year, despite a host of mitigating factors beyond the school's control, not to mention the educator's own professional opposition to such a bankrupt educational goal. In her 2014 story for the *New Yorker* chronicling the circumstances surrounding the Atlanta test-cheating scandal, journalist Rachel Aviv captures how otherwise dedicated and ethical educators were put in the position of choosing whether to allow their students to be displaced, as several years of low test scores would lead to the school's closure, or if they should make changes to their students' answer sheets (I discuss this case further in chapter 5).[13] Many educators chose the latter and ended up in court, many of them convicted.

I don't condone cheating (or lying, for that matter!), but I unequivocally condemn the system that led those teachers—and countless others across the country—to feel they had to choose between two terrible options. While the Atlanta judge who convicted the accused educators (all of them African American) described their actions as "criminal," Aviv's reporting captures a more nuanced story, one in which at least some of those involved took great risks to do what they believed was best for their students. No doubt it is also true that some of the educators involved were guilty of simply protecting their own jobs. Even so, the Atlanta case is a clear illustration of how high-stakes testing does much more to make cheaters out of both honest and errant practitioners than it does to improve anyone's teaching or learning.

When educators who care about their school and their kids are expected to suspend their own judgment in order to carry out plans they believe harm their students, cheating and deflection are a natural outcome. During my time as a teacher, I learned that if we wanted to avoid creating a culture of deception in the schools I helped start, my colleagues and I would have to build a school culture based on trust and support—one in which both disagreement and even outright resistance could be expressed openly and honestly.

For example, one Mission Hill School teacher believed strongly that the state MCAS (Massachusetts Comprehensive Assessment System) test, which became mandated in 1999 (a year after MHS opened), was harmful to children and useless for teachers (especially at that time when schools didn't get results back until the following year). Based on his conviction, he refused to administer the MCAS to his fourth- and fifth-grade students. Actually, most of our families had opted out of having their child tested, so it was just a handful of kids who would be taking it. (Emily goes into detail about the MHS community's response to standardized testing in chapter 4.) Several staff members felt that the teacher should proctor the test out of respect for families who had chosen to have their children sit for it. But he felt strongly that doing so would be more of a compromise than he was willing to make. In the end, the staff agreed to let him stay home on testing days while someone else on staff administered the test to students. It was far from being a perfect solution, but it was one that we were able to discuss and argue over, and we were able to come to a decision that everyone could live with.

Democracy requires that we be able to navigate complexity, that we make decisions under circumstances in which there may be multiple possible solutions, or, indeed, only the better of two or more bad options. In schools that serve democracy, adults model such decision making for students. It is also our responsibility as democratic educators to provide students with a learning environment that fosters the development of each individual's sense of identity and personal standards.

But with strong identity and individual standards comes great responsibility. We adults—educators and families—must explicitly discuss with children how to thoughtfully reconcile their own needs and values with the myriad different sets of norms, expectations, and, of course, prejudices they will encounter as they move through the world, from one setting to another. At Central Park East elementary school, teachers explained to children why they should walk in silent, straight lines when passing through the halls of the more traditional middle school whose facility we shared, even though in their own school they were expected to manage themselves when they walked through the halls.

At Central Part East Secondary School, we regularly discussed with our predominantly Black and Brown students how to interact with those in positions of authority, including law enforcement, while remaining rooted in their own sense of self, which was often seen as a threat by said authorities. In these cases, we taught them that they had the right to resist by withholding information about themselves that they thought might be used in a way that was not in their best interest. I regularly gave students the opportunity to practice this form of silent resistance to authority by explaining to them that they should not tell me (the authority in that case) anything that they didn't want me to share with their families or outside agencies because I had a responsibility as principal to exercise such judgment if I believed I could not legally or ethically keep what they told me to myself. At bottom, this ongoing discussion we had with children was about how to exercise sound judgment—how to go forth and be bold, but not foolish; how to courageously yet safely respond to trespasses against their identities, in whatever form that took, in ways that took into account the level of risk associated with different settings.

FOSTERING A CULTURE OF TRUST

While few traditional schools encourage enough of the kind of open exchange described in the previous section, the level of student freedom to voice opinions tends to increase in accordance with the student body's socioeconomic status, with schools that serve a predominantly poor population often severely limiting student expression to canned content. It's as if we do not trust children from poor communities to develop and express their own ideas. This stance can take a particularly pernicious form when schools enlist the help of modern technology in this ignoble cause, creating surveillance technologies replete with hidden cameras, locker searches, and police patrols roaming the corridors, and relentlessly excluding those who resist. Even though the lion's share of student-initiated school violence over the past twenty-five years has been carried out in majority-white schools (beginning with the Columbine High School massacre and most recently at Sandy Hook Elementary School), police-state security has *only* increased in schools that serve more than 50 percent students of color.[14] The National Association of School Psychologists, along with numerous scholars and educators, warns that heightened security measures negatively impact a school's learning environment and undermine the fundamental relationships between adults and children, making it impossible to nurture the degree of trust and respect that should characterize all schools in a democracy.[15]

Through my experience starting democratically governed schools, I have come to understand the importance of creating systems and structures that support open, honest resistance from all constituents—students, teachers, families, and even administrators, who must be in a position to resist external mandates that threaten the integrity of the school culture. Interestingly, over the years, I have found myself drawn to teachers who have been considered "troublemakers," many of them (including Emily!) had even been fired from their former schools for being such. But with each school that I helped start—first, the Central Park East and Coalition Schools in New York City, and then, Mission Hill School in Boston—I gained insight into how to better work with staff to establish cultural norms that encourage healthy disagreement and pushback. We set up forums in which members of the school community were invited to air their grievances and share their ideas for improvement; we kept the school community small enough that everyone could come to know and feel known by everyone else; we created formal tools to facilitate a peer-review process that involved teachers and colleagues from sister schools and universities providing one another with critical feedback.

At Mission Hill School, we required that, upon accepting a position, teachers agree to meet together regularly to identify and hash out solutions for an array of problems that invariably arise in the daily operation of a school. We became more intentional about setting up structures that would make visible the nearly constant negotiations involved in establishing and sustaining a well-functioning community—it was imperative that teachers see their administrators push back against external mandates and that students see their teachers engaged in discussions, sometimes heated, generally passionate, about how to address long- and short-term questions of practice.

The bottom line is, if we are ever going to fulfill the promise for schools to become incubators for democracy, then that task requires creating a democratic adult culture within the schools themselves that mirrors the one we want for children. For if we expect the young to grow into judicious citizens and thoughtful, competent stewards in matters of national and global welfare, then it only makes sense that we start by trusting local constituents—students, parents, teachers, and neighbors—to weigh in on and make decisions concerning the serious matters that affect their lives in school.

Unfortunately, the last two decades of education reform have increasingly been characterized by a disconnect between the original purpose of education and anything remotely resembling foundational ideas about democracy. As a sign of the times, over the past ten years or so, I have noticed a trend in the kinds of questions audience members tend to ask after my talks. Invariably, a teacher or principal stands up and urges me to share my thoughts on what the way forward might be—where, in my travels across the education landscape, have I found glimmers of hope for democratic education? Sometimes they tell about their own struggles, attempting to find cracks in which to do authentic work with children in rigid school settings or fighting to keep alive the vision in a small, progressive school amidst myriad pressures to conform to some uninspired norm. Sometimes they ask a question simply to gain some sense of connection with like-minded practitioners in order to stay afloat professionally because they are losing steam or heart, or both.

I try to respond with optimism—there are indeed great public schools, new and established, rural and urban, in-system and charter sprinkled across the country. But regardless of a school's values, vision, or organization, all face multiple obstacles to staying true to their underlying mission of public purpose. Most significantly, the unrelenting pressure to tie everything they do to student test scores, in conjunction with a growing disregard for the professional knowledge of educators, makes it near impossible for democratic (and other, otherwise innovative) schools to "hold values."[16] As a result, many great schools are being closed or mandated to employ more standardized practices and our most creative and inspired educators are leaving the public schools or education altogether, out of frustration.

What policies would reverse this trend? In a 2016 report by the Learning Policy Institute, the researchers cite conditions in schools as the primary factor influencing teachers' decision of whether or not to leave the profession.[17] In particular, the authors explain, "Accountability pressures focused on test preparation and leading to sanctions comprised the most frequently cited area of dissatisfaction, listed by 25% of teachers who left." Clearly, policies that placed less emphasis on the production of and outcomes from numeric data would be a good first step in the right direction. Unfortunately, we live in a time when, despite widespread acknowledgement at all levels that standardized testing is "sucking all the oxygen out of the room," as former secretary of education Arne Duncan ironically proclaimed in 2014, there has been a continuation, if not an intensification, of policies that require schools to value numeric data over human judgment.[18]

Human judgment being at the heart of democratic practice in and beyond schools, this current state of affairs regarding mistrust of educators and an over-reliance on external "experts" (or, indeed, on those with business expertise in place of education experience), and the data they demand and produce leaves us with a fundamental conundrum. How can we hope to educate for democracy if children and the adults in their lives never have the opportunity to observe or practice it? And if such an education doesn't take place in our public schools, then where will it happen?

CHAPTER 2

FALLING FOR DEMOCRACY

A YOUNG TEACHER'S EDUCATION

Emily Gasoi

> If I am not in the world simply to adapt to it, but rather
> transform it, and if it is not possible to change the world
> without a certain dream or vision for it, I must make use
> of every possibility there is not only to speak about my
> utopia, but also to engage in practices consistent with it.
>
> —PAULO FREIRE, 2004[1]

"I NEVER THOUGHT ABOUT the connection between democracy and education before reading this essay." This response kicked off our discussion of one of Deborah's essays that I had assigned in a course I was teaching for candidates enrolled in a progressive teacher-training program. The individual who responded was Norah, a particularly engaged student and promising teacher in her twenties. I was not surprised by Norah's comment, or by the many hands that went up when I asked who else had a similar revelation upon reading Deborah's essay.

In 2004, after living and teaching in Boston for ten years, I had moved to Washington, DC, and enrolled in a doctoral program a year later. After my graduate studies, I began working as a course instructor and mentor for in-service and first-year teachers. Removed from the small, progressive education bubble I'd been part of in Boston, I came to the understanding that, despite her near rock-star status among old-school progressives, Deborah was fairly unknown in mainstream education circles. In many of the courses I taught, I found that, though my students were versed in the literature on progressive pedagogy, very few of the mostly millennial teaching candidates had read much about the connection between education and democracy.

Even so, the irony of the situation with Norah was not lost on me. Earlier in the course, I had asked the students to write a personal essay situating their emerging professional practice within their own experiences as K–12 students. In her essay, Norah wrote that she had grown up in a middle-class family, that she had attended "good" public elementary schools and prestigious private middle and high schools, and that she had been a straight-A student on through college. Despite Norah's educational advantages, she had not, in her sixteen or so years of schooling, been asked to consider the relationship between her time in school and her responsibilities as a citizen in a democratic society—not in a memorable way, in any case. And then I had to ask myself, *Had my experience as a student been any different?*

I had *not* always gone to what I would call good schools and I had been bored through much of my schooling. But, like Norah, I don't remember anything in my many years as a student that made me think about my education in relation to my rights and responsibilities as a citizen in a democratic society. The closest thing I can think of was my two years in Head Start, where our teachers taught us to take care of one another, especially the most vulnerable among us.[2] But that spirit was shredded once we entered the traditional K–12 school in my town. I do remember my eighth-grade social studies teacher handing out Solidarity buttons for students to wear to support Poland's early-1980s anti-communism movement, but I don't recall the teacher asking us to think about what it meant to transition from a totalitarian to a democratic regime. I just knew that the United States had a democratic form of government and therefore we were supposed to root for democracy.

Thus, Norah's revelation led me to a revelation of my own, which was that, before going to work at Mission Hill School (MHS) over ten years earlier, I hadn't thought much about the connection between democracy and education either. In fact, by the time I began having my own ideas about issues of equity and social justice at some point during high school, democracy had become a hollow word, as it had for many of my generation.

I came of age during the Reagan revolution, the only era in recent history in which young adults were likely to hold more conservative values than their parents. However, this wasn't true in my case. My mother was a political activist who proudly told me that I had attended my first antiwar demonstration in utero. I walked on my own two feet in numerous actions throughout my adolescence, from protesting violent media images against women to opposing America's covert wars in Central America.

Regardless of whether you fought for peace and justice or for lower taxes and deregulation, however, by the late 1980s, "democracy" had become a broad and abstract notion. For the Reagan youth, the democratic imperative lost steam with the end of the Cold War and became conflated with free-market economics. For my left-leaning peers, it was an empty word that we'd come to associate with politicians' disingenuous excuses for micromanaging the political and economic aspirations of sovereign nations around the globe.

In my own progressive teacher-training program at the Shady Hill School in Cambridge, Massachusetts, we learned that the original purpose of universal education was to ensure that our then fledgling democracy would be sustained by a populace that was, if not socially or economically equal, at least equally educated. But we also learned that public schools were designed according to a factory model and that early "school men" had seen the common school as the ideal place to sort students into tracks based on the rank they'd best serve in society. Not surprisingly, these tracks almost always fell along race and class lines. Knowing the history of systemic inequity in our country (in part perpetuated through continued tracking along socioeconomic and race lines, even in schools that, on paper, are "diverse"), I took this aspiration with a grain of salt as well.

Even when I read Deborah's first book, *The Power of Their Ideas,* before starting at Mission Hill School, it wasn't the idea of education for democracy that resonated with me so much as what Deborah had proven through twenty-plus years in the field: that it is possible to provide for all children the kind of well-rounded, intellectually powerful education usually reserved for a privileged few. Before my experience working in a democratically governed school, I had not understood equity and democracy as necessarily twinned, as they were in Deborah's vision of schools.

When I moved to Washington in 2004, the full impact of No Child Left Behind and other high-stakes reforms were just beginning to be felt nationwide, fostering in millions of schools a culture of intense stress over raising students' test scores in two academic subjects and compelling principals to cut "extras," such as art, recess, phys ed, and, in some cases, even social studies and science. Mission Hill School met its first big challenge during those years, but by then the staff had a strong foundation on which to base our convictions.

Now that I work with young teachers who are coming into the profession with the current reform climate as their primary frame of reference and with a very slim chance of working in a school organized around democratic values and practices, I can't help echo the concern Deborah expresses in the previous chapter—*how can we hope to educate children for democracy if they and the adults in their lives have never really experienced it?*

While history offers those who know to look for it some insight into the connection between free, universal education and democratic citizenship, as Norah and my experience make clear, it's entirely possible to go through the better part of two decades of schooling without ever being asked to consider this aspect of our education. Given this, it is vital, now more than ever, that this generation of educators knows what is possible for school to look and feel like.

AN EDUCATION

I had only been teaching for two years when Deborah Meier came to Boston in 1997 to embark on her fifth and final adventure starting a new school. News of her arrival caused a stir among many of my colleagues in the small, progressive private school where we worked just outside the city. One veteran teacher whom I looked to as a mentor, Heidi Lyne, recommended that I read *The Power of Their Ideas*, Deborah's recently published book about her highly acclaimed Central Park East schools in New York. After reading it, I was determined to work at her new school. I liked my position well enough, teaching a mixed-age third-and-fourth-grade classroom in a project-based private school where teachers and students had a significant degree of freedom to shape curriculum according to our collective and emergent interests. But, though all children deserve an education that empowers them to follow their passions, build on their strengths, and grapple with important decisions, the emphasis that Deborah placed on creating such powerful learning opportunities in a public school setting resonated powerfully with me, as this was my primary motivation for pursuing a career in education.

Shortly after deciding to apply for a teaching position at what would become the Mission Hill School, I encountered some serious obstacles. First, I learned that Deborah only hired teachers with a minimum of three years' experience. I thought perhaps I would stay another year in my private school position and then apply the following year as MHS grew. But then, with no warning, I was fired. My principal never gave me a solid reason. In the meeting in which she informed me she would not renew my contract, she mumbled something about how it was unusual for such a new teacher to speak up as much as I did in faculty meetings. But that was the extent of her rationale. In the meantime, my colleague Heidi was also let go, for similarly mysterious reasons. Heidi was vindicated a few weeks later, becoming the first teacher hired at Deborah's new school. With only two years' experience and a bruised professional ego, I decided to apply to MHS as an assistant teacher.

When I entered the room for the interview, I saw six individuals seated in a small circle of chairs. I recognized two people in the group: one, of course, was my former colleague Heidi, who had been hired to teach a mixed-age classroom of seven- and eight-year-olds; the other, a woman in her late sixties whom I knew from the picture on the dust jacket of her book, was Deborah Meier. A young African American man named Brian introduced himself as Deborah's assistant, in training to become the assistant principal, and he gestured for me to take a seat in the circle. The other three people also introduced themselves: Alicia, an African American woman, and Geralyn, a white woman, both in their late twenties, would each teach one of two classes of five- and six-year-olds; Angel, a Latino man in his early thirties, would teach the only classroom of nine- and ten-year-olds.[3] And so it went, with the entire (albeit, tiny) staff taking part in the interview. In addition to looking for assistant teachers, they told me, they were also searching for one last lead teacher for the second classroom of seven- and eight-year-olds.

Usually the most that one can hope for when applying for a new job is to be chosen for the position for which one has applied. My career at MHS started with a most unusual offer. Although I had presented myself as a candidate for a classroom assistant position, when Deborah called me the next day, she offered me the last lead teacher position. I would come to understand that this experience was indicative of two important qualities about the school.

First, MHS was a place of possibility. If someone—a teacher, student, parent, or custodian—had an idea, there would be a forum in which to pitch it. As part of a staff-governed school, Deborah, Brian, and the teachers would hear a proposal, then discuss and often argue over it. Some proposals, for various reasons, were quickly tabled or dissolved into endless discussion. But the staff put many proposals into action, such as Paul the custodian's idea to turn portions of the school yard into flower and vegetable plots; a group of parents' suggestion to turn an otherwise underutilized common space into a library (Deborah had originally imagined that we would just use the public library a few blocks away); the K–1 team's proposal to have the school's oldest students run the Friday assembly; and the suggestion from Angel, the fourth-fifth-grade teacher, to store some of our works in progress on tables and walls in the hallway, so students could see one another's projects evolve over time.

Second, I came to understand that Deborah had a soft spot when it came to hiring people who had been fired from previous positions (in fact, three of the five teachers on staff, including Heidi and me, had been let go more than once). This was not an intentional act of rebellion on Deborah's part. When she opened a school she didn't write a job posting explicitly calling for people who had broken rules or who had pushed back too hard against something they thought unfair or who shared their opinions a little too often in faculty meetings. But, as she said herself in the previous chapter, Deborah did tend to attract (and was no doubt drawn to) people who were generally considered "troublemakers" in more traditional settings. Her primary concern, she told new hires, was in finding "interesting" adults, both to act as role models for students (she often expressed how important it was to surround the young with adults they could imagine becoming) and to contribute to the school's rich collegial culture. That these interesting people who made their way into her company had made themselves unwelcome in other quarters seemed to please her on some level, perhaps contributing to a mischievous sense of pride.

Once the inaugural staff, consisting of two administrators, two administrative assistants, five classroom teachers, and an assistant for each class, was assembled, Deborah gave us all a copy of the proposal she had submitted for MHS to become a member of the newly formed Boston Pilot School Network (BPSN), a collaboration between the Boston Public Schools superintendent and the Boston Teachers Union that granted public schools the autonomy to innovate.[4] MHS was one of the early elementary schools to open within the fledgling BPSN, which, to a large extent, was a continuation of the work that Deborah and colleagues had started in scaling up a small-schools network in New York City (more on this in chapter 7). The pilot proposal provided us with an outline of Deborah's vision for how MHS would be structured. In her previous schools, Deborah had found that whole-school themes promoted collegiality, and so in the proposal she specified that the school year would be organized around three in-depth themes: one focused on an ancient civilization, one focused on physical or earth sciences, and one focused on a topic closer in time and space like our neighborhoods; a significant historical period, such as the civil rights movement of the 1950s–1960s or, in political campaign years, the electoral process. She also specified that in place of standardized tests, MHS would develop its own portfolio and performance assessments—some internally reviewed and others that involved the input of external reviewers—as well as specific assessments for the different subject areas. The Five Habits of Mind, which Deborah brought with her from Central Park East Secondary School, would guide our planning and work with children, and most important decisions concerning instruction, pedagogy, and school operations would be decided collectively by the staff, while more macro decisions concerning the school would be taken up by the school governance board, made up of a set number of teachers, family, community members, and, eventually, middle school students.

Deborah brought this scaffolding with her from her previous schools, but she left us, the staff, to fill in the contours and suggest changes to the framework itself. We met eight hours a day, five days a week, for close to a month, before the school opened to hammer out a curriculum, develop assessments, and plan our first days, During our off hours, we continued our "meetings" in pubs, cafes, or one another's homes. The meetings bubbled over with the anticipatory excitement of embarking on a great adventure with a band of spirited comrades. In retrospect, I realize that this intensive preparation not only set a high bar for productive collaboration but was, in and of itself, an invaluable bonding experience for the staff and laid the foundation for a culture of almost fierce collegiality.

DEMOCRATIC GOVERNANCE AND ITS AMBIGUITIES

While Deb (as I came to call her) created a framework for democratic governance, it wasn't always easy to navigate the various personality and power dynamics that inevitably arose. This was especially true when it came to interactions involving Deb. There were two realities. One was that we were all responsible for being the makers and keepers of the school culture, as well as being in charge of much of the school's daily functioning. The other reality was that Deb was always the heavyweight in the room, whether in our staff meetings or in a forum of a thousand educators. She had thirty-plus years of extraordinary experience to draw upon, By the time she came to Boston, in 1996, Deb was something of an edu-celebrity, at least among progressive educators. She had already accomplished a host of incredible professional feats: starting and helping to start scores of democratic public schools in New York City, winning a MacArthur Foundation "Genius" award, speaking and writing truth to power, and, now, opening yet another tradition-defying school in our very own city. Just being part of the MHS project made us feel like we were a team of super-star educators taking part in a dream-school tour de force.

When Deb liked an idea, or when someone raised a point that piqued her curiosity, it was like sunshine. I felt a great sense of possibility flow forth when she responded with pleasure to something one of us presented. It might just be a conversation that would become elevated due to Deb's interest—a proposal for shaking up some idea or practice we'd taken for granted, or a suggestion for solving a particular problem. And hearing Deb respond to something I had said with, "That's an interesting idea; let's play with that," filled me with an outsize sense of pride. Sometimes her interest in an idea had more concrete outcomes. I recall when, early on in our first year, one of us asked if we could offer a part-time position to Joyce Stevens, a project consultant who was initially hired just to work with us over the summer. "Can we keep her?" someone asked. I remember Deb smiling and tossing it back to the staff: "Oh, I like that idea; how can we make that happen?" The staff came up with a plan to utilize Joyce's time three days a week, and we figured out how to make it financially viable. In the end, Joyce joined us as an incredible part-time resource for years to come.

At other times, Deb's way of presenting her opinion, and her way of challenging ours, felt intimidating. She tended to ask questions with a bluntness that was at times unsettling; she could present her arguments with great intensity, and there was often what I perceived to be a rising sense of irritation rumbling beneath her rebuttals when one or even a group of us voiced disagreement. Ultimately, it was hard *not* to think of Deb as the "boss," especially in that first year, in large part because we were all new to democratic leadership but also because, even if it weren't for her position as school principal, Deb was a force—a leader among leaders. It took a concerted effort for most of us not to see her as the intrepid captain of our ship, the protector of our proud experiment and, therefore, worthy of our deference, even if she pushed against such traditional power dynamics. When Deb had an opinion, she invited us to argue with her, but it was hard for someone like me, a second-year teacher, to think of myself as her equal. As a staff, we worked within the ever-present tension of those comingling realities.

For example, a few months into the first school year, Deb came into my classroom to observe and then commended me for engaging students in solo recitations of a short poem, one after another.

Two boys, J.J. and Clarence, whom I had spoken about in staff meetings because I often had difficulty engaging them, volunteered and stood to recite the poem perfectly, an air of quiet pride surrounding their brief performances. Deb witnessed this exercise and came over to whisper in my ear, "I love your classroom." My whole being filled with light. Though we were a democratically governed school with a peer-review system intended to flatten traditional hierarchical relationships, Deb's opinion of my evolving practice still counted for a thousand more points than anyone else's. But, I would soon find, so did her *critique* of my practice.

On another occasion, not long after her first visit, Deb came into my room again, this time when the children were outside doing what MHS calls "backyard exploration."[5] I don't recall the original reason for her visit, but as she was leaving she glanced over at the daily schedule I'd written on the board. She stopped and asked me pointedly, "Why do you have all those times up there for teaching separate subjects? I thought we had all agreed that we were teaching through projects and theme work?"

Deb was right. This had been one of the primary topics of discussion during our summer retreat leading up to opening the school. We had spent entire days working out how to create integrated, thematic curricula that would allow us to teach subject-specific content and skills within a meaningful context. And teaching through projects would give students the opportunity to engage in experiential learning. Developing curriculum in this way was fundamental to the school's commitment to constructivist learning theory and progressive philosophy of education. It was also part of our Boston Pilot School Network agreement.

I was wholly enthusiastic about the idea of teaching this way. But to my own surprise, when it came time to set up my class routines and plan my integrated, project-based, thematic lessons, I was at a loss. As a fairly new teacher, I found that I wasn't quite ready to change the practices I had just begun to feel comfortable with at the private school where I had previously worked. In my first two years of teaching, I had grown accustomed to having freedom to innovate and, to a limited degree, to develop integrated lessons. But at my old school, curriculum integration was considered a plus, something teachers were free to do when they felt it made most sense, whereas at MHS, curriculum integration was essential to the school's mission.

And, also to my surprise, I didn't yet feel comfortable admitting that I was having trouble. Despite the bonds I'd formed with my colleagues over the summer, the strong culture of trust that would eventually evolve was still inchoate, at least for me. So, I set up my MHS classroom more or less as I had in my previous school. In the morning, we rotated through academic subjects—reading, writing, and math. In the afternoon, we had a two-hour block during which students worked on theme-related projects. We also had class meetings, time for quiet reading and reading aloud, and music and art specials sprinkled throughout the schedule.

When Deb questioned me about the discrete subject periods on my schedule, my immediate reaction was to feel ashamed. I knew that I had agreed to teach more holistically. During our summer retreat, each classroom teacher had shared initial plans for bringing to life for students our first schoolwide theme: studying the community around the school. I had presented my plan for studying the native plants and geology (the neighborhood was known for its impressive outcroppings of puddingstone) and the "Three Sister" crops—squash, beans, and maize—that the native Massachusett people would have planted in our area.

As part of my presentation, I had elaborated on the clear opportunities for integrating all academic subjects into this approach to our theme work: Students would study earth science both through our geology research and by tending an indoor garden (as a staff, we budgeted $200 for each teacher to spend as we saw fit, and I had used part of mine to purchase a grow lab kit that I built for the classroom). They would use multiplication and division for numerous tasks, including drawing up plans for outdoor garden plots, which we would plant in the spring, and figuring out how to fairly distribute materials and the bounty from our plants once it was time to harvest. They would then apply measurement skills to scale down their outdoor plans to fit in our classroom and for tracking plant growth. They also would have science journals in which to record their observations and findings from their science study, and, of course, they would read and write about the history of our neighborhood's natural environment and changes in the population over time.

And this was the plan, more or less, that was unfolding in my classroom each afternoon during our two-hour project block. I thought it was going well, and yet Deb's question—"Why do you have all those times up there for teaching separate subjects?"— made me feel as if I'd been caught doing something wrong. Just as I was elated by her earlier approval, what I perceived as her disapproval knocked the wind out of me.

I don't recall exactly how I responded to her question, but I think I said something about the schedule working for the kids and me. What *is* vivid in my mind is that I felt even more defensive when Deb suggested that I observe in other classrooms. I wanted to say (but didn't) that I wasn't the only one doing things this way! I knew that at least one of my colleagues was also breaking up part of the day into discrete subject periods. But I'm sure Deb *also* knew that, which is probably why she suggested that I raise the issue at the next curriculum meeting that I was to facilitate, to see how others were actualizing our school plan.

At that point in the life of our school, our curriculum meetings had focused on what we *were* doing in our respective classrooms. Sharing the question that Deb had raised, about how I organized my day, would shift the conversation to what I, in particular, *wasn't* doing. It would also require me to share my anxiety around my inexperience teaching a fully integrated curriculum. Despite my reservations, I followed Deb's advice. At the next curriculum meeting, I asked my colleagues to share how they organized their theme-based work. It turned out that we were all approaching the school plan quite differently.

Alicia, who taught K–1, had a similar schedule to my own, while Angel, who taught the fourth-fifth graders, had decided not to follow our schoolwide theme at all but to allow the curriculum to emerge from students' interests. Sometimes this fit with what the rest of the school was doing, such as when some students decided to build dollhouses modeled after the neighborhood architecture. Heidi, my grade-level partner, and Geralyn, the other K–1 teacher, were the only two teachers following the original plan we had all agreed to: they were integrating all subjects into theme work that took place throughout the morning and often carried over into the afternoon after lunch.

That meeting was the first of many on this topic, as we worked together over the course of the year to clarify our collective norms around curriculum and a whole host of other defining structures and practices. Through discussion, observing in one another's rooms, and sharing research and resources, most of us concluded that teaching an integrated curriculum through an extended morning project time helped to create cross-pollination (students could visit other classes to get ideas or share supplies during project time; also, projects often spilled out into the wide corridor—by design—so kids could see what the other classrooms were working on). We also agreed that the morning was when we were all—students and teachers—most awake and alert, and was therefore the best time to focus on our theme work. We felt strongly that these common practices helped build a cohesive culture around sharing our works-in-progress. Only Angel disagreed with this plan. He continued to engage students in emergent curriculum.

This presented us with one of the fundamental dilemmas with which democracy requires us to wrestle, that is, balancing individual needs with those of the larger community. Angel had managed to become the nonconformist in a school that generally celebrated nonconformity. Within this context, Angel seemed to be within his right to stand his ground regarding his insistence on teaching emergent curriculum. Deb was not inherently against emergent curriculum—in fact, she pointed out that Angel would have fit in at the Central Park East elementary schools, where emergent curriculum was the norm. But before opening MHS we had all agreed that we would do schoolwide themes, and so having one classroom be the exception threw a wrench into the plan.

So, Deb expressed her concern over Angel's lone-wolf approach and encouraged the rest of us to voice our thoughts on the matter. But it was an uncomfortable situation, which is something we would learn Deb never shied away from. In the end, Angel ended up leaving mid-year, in part out of exhaustion from attempting to keep up with a very demanding mode of teaching in a school where there wasn't the support system to facilitate it. Deb and I have since puzzled over whether there might have been a way to allow for more variety in how we taught and if we might have provided Angel with more support. Democratic decision making is filled with dilemmas and trade-offs, and this situation with Angel was a particularly dramatic example.

But before Angel made the decision for us, I think my colleagues and I secretly hoped that Deb would just take on the role of a traditional principal in this case and tell Angel what to do.

Breaking out of these hierarchical roles with Deb depended so much on her awareness and her determination to do so.[6] Throughout our first year together, I think Deb found herself continually swatting questions we instinctually directed to her back to the whole staff and reminding us to see one another as co-authorities, allies, experts. She also had to remind us that not only was it acceptable for us to push back when we disagreed with her or with one another but also that it was vital to the development of our democratic culture that we do so. And though I sometimes grew defensive when she questioned my decisions, I soon came to understand that Deb was modeling the kind of constructive but critical stance she was hoping we would all take toward one another's work. Ultimately, being able to honestly critique one another's practice turned out to be one of the greatest challenges we faced as a staff—one we never felt satisfied that we fully surmounted.

At some point during the ongoing discussion about thematic teaching, I remember explaining to Deb how her question about my schedule had initially upset me. She was glad that I'd told her, but she also expressed frustration that it was often difficult to engage one another in critical feedback. She explained that if we were to have a democratically governed school, then we all had to be open to questioning one another, especially concerning matters we didn't understand or with which we disagreed. I thought about how I had lapped up her compliment but then recoiled at what I had interpreted as her disapproval. In fact, I felt that the one canceled out the other, which, of course, wasn't true.

What I came to understand was that Deb experienced the life of the school as a living current, an ever-evolving work that existed most potently in the interactions between its constituents. Further, she saw disagreement as a healthy part of that communication, and she herself thrived on what most others experienced as discomforting conflict. While I initially interpreted her comment about my decision as a professional rebuff, she saw it as an invitation to discussion and, therefore, an equally, if not more, important interaction than her earlier compliment of my classroom culture.

I think it's fair to say that when I began working at MHS, I understood our school's mission, to "help . . . raise youngsters who will maintain and nurture the best habits of a democratic society" on an intellectual level.[7] But it took time for me to fully bridge the gap between the false rhetorical notion of democracy I had perceived throughout my youth and early adulthood and Deb's vision of democratic practices as the means *and* the end in the struggle for a more just society.

Through grappling with difficult, often uncomfortable situations, such as the one involving Deb's challenge to my class schedule, our loss of a valued staff member, and many, many more, I began to understand and eventually respond to Deb's insistence that classroom teachers, as those closest to students and families, should take part in making most of the important decisions in our school. Over time, I came to see that the depth of professional autonomy and the level of respect and trust my colleagues and I enjoyed in our work mirrored what we hoped for all our students. In other words, at MHS we practiced and lived values that we strove to see in society more broadly. And if we hoped for such a future, then our students would have to be the ones to forge it, which is why Deb insisted on "schooling for ruling" for all children and that public schools should be the primary setting "where ordinary people learn the trade of democracy—its particular body of knowledge, its particular skills, its 'habits of mind.'"[8]

CHAPTER 3

FALLING FOR PUBLIC EDUCATION

A HOTHOUSE FOR DEMOCRACY

Deborah Meier

> Let the young soul survey its own life with a view of the
> following question: "What have you truly loved thus far?
> What has ever uplifted your soul, what has dominated
> and delighted it at the same time?" Assemble these re-
> vered objects in a row before you and perhaps they will
> reveal a law by their nature and their order: the funda-
> mental law of your very self.
>
> —FRIEDRICH NIETZSCHE
> in *Schopenhauer as Educator*[1]

WHEN I BEGAN SUBBING IN 1963, I did so in part to supplement
my husband's income, but mostly out of political curiosity. I approached my year going in and out of a slew of mostly grim classrooms on Chicago's South Side as a sociologist might, interested
in gaining some insight into the inequities I knew existed in public schooling. I intended it to be a short-term gig. I couldn't have
imagined then that education would become my life's journey.

In the world I grew up in, women were generally confined to
teaching, nursing, and secretarial jobs. I (and those closest to me)
had me pegged for what we imagined were greater things. I was
raised in an intellectually and politically vibrant household. My

father was executive director of the Federation of Jewish Philanthropies, and my mother was active in myriad social and political causes, including running for city council, and I was sure I'd follow in their footsteps (though for a time I secretly dreamed of writing the next "great American novel"). Because of my parents' involvements, a retinue of prominent intellectuals, artists, political leaders, and activists flowed in and out of our home. Counting these experiences as an integral part of my education, I supposed I was expected to join in their conversations and, eventually, their ranks.

The private school my brother and I attended when we moved into New York City in 1939, Ethical Culture Fieldston School, emphasized cultivating in students the dispositions and skills we would need to become competent and engaged citizens—or as they put it, "the leaders of our democracy." Intellectually, I thrived in this environment, where we were expected to formulate our own opinions, ideas, and solutions related to the social-political-scientific issues swirling around us. By high school I had gained recognition from teachers and peers alike for possessing an aptitude for argument on almost any topic.

An inescapable factor influencing my commitment to democratic ideals was what I consider my doubly privileged upbringing. I was privileged because I was white and my family had the means and position to provide me access to useful networks. But I also feel that I was privileged to participate in their adult world, to shape my own opinions, and to challenge those with whom I disagreed, both at home and at school.

In my household, the dinner table became an important training ground for adulthood, where we children got to listen to and eventually join in adult talk. My particular aptitude for the art of argument I learned from my father, who was considered by all who knew him to be almost allergic to agreement. My father was fond of telling us about how, around *his* family dinner table, his parents routinely engaged him and his siblings in long, sometimes heated and contentious discussions that went on long after they'd finished eating. His father even accused him of being "disrespectful" when my father grew tired of debating and began agreeing too often.

This family respect for argument was handed down, from one generation to the next. Whether meeting with potential donors, entertaining the political and cultural luminaries who frequented my family's West Side apartment, or alone with us, my father provoked arguments, often defending multiple sides of a given dispute. His penchant for argument for its own sake was, of course, often frustrating and did not lend itself to what scholar Amy Gutmann calls "deliberative democracy." Still, my father's provocations helped me to see contradictions as a normal, even inevitable part of life by showing me the truth inherent in multiple sides of things.

It was my mother's work and values, however, that led me to view democracy both as a means and an end for moving toward a more just and equitable society. A victim of her time and class, she never had a paying job, though she held a graduate degree in social work. Nevertheless, she was a talented political leader and tirelessly fought against injustices she believed threatened democratic values at their core on an unpaid basis. My mother led several influential women's groups, including the Council for Jewish Women, and was a cofounder of the New York City Labor Party and later the Liberal Party, where she struggled to hold her ground as one of the few women leaders among men. She also wrote a regular column for a local labor union newspaper and ran for city council on the Liberal Party ticket. Ironically, given that she herself never earned a salary, in 1963 she and other women leaders were invited to pose with President Kennedy as he signed the Equal Pay Act into law. (My granddaughter Sarah recently uncovered the photo of the event with amazement and pride.)

But beyond my family and my formal education, I am also a product of my time, or my perception of that time. In my memory of growing up in New York City during the New Deal era, talk of democracy was part of the fabric of our everyday lives—it resonated throughout the speeches of prominent political figures, union leaders, and activists; it came pulsing through the airwaves in popular songs; and, eventually, it resounded in the booming rhetoric that buoyed us through the Second World War.

When I was ten years old, President Roosevelt's 1941 State of the Union address, which we listened to on the radio, framed America's impending involvement in the war under the banner of democracy and the Four Freedoms: freedom of speech, freedom of worship, freedom from want, and freedom from fear.[2] I vividly remember how the clarity of his words and the resolution in his voice stirred me and filled me with a sense of outsize pride at being part of something bigger than myself.

While my parents were both engaged in causes that exposed me to some of the most dramatic injustices of our time, I now realize that throughout much of my childhood, I probably had an overly rosy view of things. For example, I remember spending several happy prewar summers at the Southern School for Workers (SSW) in Asheville, North Carolina, a resident workers' school that my mother helped organize. The school brought together Black and white workers to organize for their common interest in gaining better conditions for workers of all races, and based on the multiple hardships and hurdles the members had to fight, I'm sure there were also multiple tensions at play. But my experience of SSW was characterized by what seemed to me to be easy interracial intermingling untypical of the time, punctuated by lots of powerful solidarity songs.

As I grew older, I became increasingly aware of the thinness inherent in FDR's rhetoric, evidenced by the ongoing injustices in my own country, many committed in the name of "fighting the good fight." Because of my father's position, we were aware, for example, of the Roosevelt administration's decision to turn back a ship full of desperate Jews fleeing Europe—for the good of the nation, it was said. Not long after came the wartime internment of Japanese Americans, which the country very belatedly admitted was a wrongdoing. We've been slower doing the same for many others. And it hardly bears mentioning that Americans, like many others, lived in a fluctuating state of contradiction between proclaimed ideals and reality regarding equity and freedom for all. Even in 1942, as we geared up for a war to protect our democratic values at home, American fighting units were segregated by race and, to a large extent, by class, with the children of the wealthy more likely to serve in the safer upper echelons of their units. It took a threatened march on Washington to end discrimination in war factories.

Even taking these factors into account, however, and looking back from our current vantage point in which democracy is more likely to be defined as respect for free-market values, I do believe that my memory of the prominent place that the *idea* of democracy took in our collective national psyche is more than just misguided nostalgia. While the Great Recession of 2008 seems to have had a relatively small impact on the public's trust of markets, when I was growing up, it was widely understood that it was the excesses of the market that had plunged the country into the decade-long Depression. There were some free-market groups within government and at the grassroots level that fought against New Deal policies, but they were a small minority, generally seen as far outside the mainstream of the time. Perhaps most importantly, the policies of the New Deal gave the rhetoric of the time some teeth—social programs that expanded the middle class through living wages, support for labor unions, home-ownership assistance, and the GI Bill, among others. Of course, the lifelines that the New Deal programs extended to many white citizens were much less accessible to Black citizens, thus undermining full realization of the programs' purpose—and thus entrenching and normalizing racial segregation in Northern cities while failing to protect Southern Blacks from legally sanctioned Jim Crow laws. The racial dimensions of the 2008 crisis were more insidious, with African American families overrepresented among those swindled out of their wealth by Wall Street real estate and savings scams.

By the time I graduated high school in 1949, the all-for-one spirit that I had felt defined my formative years was much less apparent. I witnessed America retreat into more personal and family-centered concerns, seeking a sense of normalcy that included pushing women back into their roles as homemakers. This trend intensified through the 1950s, one of the many fuse lines leading to the powder keg of social unrest that has come to define the following two decades. Perhaps my enduring and dogged fight for sentiments and policies that today seem passé, or even naïve, is rooted in these early experiences and the optimism that characterized those heady postwar years.

As I headed off to college, I followed in my brother Paul's footsteps by becoming a "revolutionary" socialist. At seventeen, I joined the Socialist Youth League, the youth organization of a Trotskyite group called the Independent Socialist League. Our modest goal was to end all injustice. All, maybe a thousand, of us organized boycotts against institutions that maintained segregationist policies, and we picketed with striking union members from various trades. As small as we were, the ISL membership included many significant writers and labor activists such as Irving Howe, Michael Harrington, James T. Farrell, and Paul Goodman; they and other writers and thinkers greatly influenced my values in those formative years.

AN EDUCATION

In 1949, I went off to Antioch College, in Yellow Springs, Ohio, which I chose because it was one of the only colleges at that time that didn't have different rules for men and women. Two years later I transferred to the University of Chicago, attracted by the lure of living in a big city again and what I perceived as the school's prestige as a center of intellectual life. In the ensuing years, I earned an MA in history; met my husband, Fred Meier; and had three children. We moved our family to Kenwood, a diverse neighborhood wedged between a dense, impoverished Black neighborhood to the north and the University of Chicago's prestigious Hyde Park to the south (a young community organizer, Barack Obama, would settle in Kenwood many decades later). We occupied one of the row houses on a street overlooking Shoesmith, our local public school, and a field and playground where I ended up spending plenty of time observing my own and other children, mostly children of color, immersed in lively, often intricate and sophisticated play.

Shoesmith School, where all three of my children soon went, was remarkable for numerous reasons, but the first thing that struck me was how integrated it was. Unlike the mostly segregated schools throughout Chicago, Shoesmith was located such that it was the zoned school for students from three demographically distinct neighborhoods: about 60 percent poor Black students, 20 percent middle-class white students, and about 20 percent wealthy Black students. Without knowing much more about education beyond that it should be public and open to all, I valued integration for both personal and political reasons.

In addition to parenting, I followed in my mother's activist footsteps and dedicated considerable time and energy to local political groups. I cochaired the NAACP's Housing Committee on issues around public housing and urban renewal. We were fighting the University of Chicago's attempt to expand its borders and repopulate its surrounding areas with wealthier and whiter residents. Around the same time, I joined the Congress of Racial Equality and became involved in designing a neighborhood community center. CORE hoped to attract young, Black civil rights workers to operate a center that would provide expert advice on housing, employment, and legal issues; provide space for organizing; and operate a drop-in child-care center for local residents.

Despite my strong connection to the neighborhood and my commitment to the community work in which I was engaged, I began to feel increasingly uneasy about my role in the civil rights groups I had joined. The interracial spirit of the Selma march (in which I took part) was entering its intense Black Power stage.[3]

Accustomed to confidently voicing my opinions at home, I often found myself pushing back on ideas presented by other, mostly Black group members, and speaking up whether the content of what I had to say was popular or not. I began to feel unsure of how useful I could be and of how I, as a white woman, came across in these forums. I held onto my interracial, integrationist vision, but my role in helping to actualize that vision was becoming unclear to me.

It was during this time of soul-searching and unsettled footing that some of my political focus began to transfer, at first by accident, to the field of public education. It started with my decision to do some substitute teaching in local public schools—an easy way, I thought, to make some extra cash and investigate Chicago's system of public education. I enrolled at the Chicago Teachers College and earned the necessary credits (partly through TV courses, a precursor to the now ubiquitous remote learning!). Once my coursework was complete, I spent three days a week in one or another all-Black, K–8 school on the city's notoriously poor and segregated South Side. Classroom management, which was at the heart of subbing, was not my forte. And the almost uniform oppressiveness of the schools I entered was shocking. Nevertheless I found the overall experience of subbing fascinating; it was an exercise in navigating an environment where there didn't seem to be enough respect or dignity to go around.

Some of the practices that belittled teachers were subtle. I was annoyed when the bureaucrats at central office referred to me as Deborah, while I knew that administrators (almost all men) were generally addressed by their surnames. But other demeaning gestures were more overt. One day I managed to involve a classroom of upper elementary-age children in a debate over a topic, now lost to me, that elicited some passionate exchanges. An administrator suddenly burst into the room and slammed the door behind him, shocking us all into silence. He went on to loudly reprimand the children for their unruly behavior and then left, as abruptly as he had come, without saying a word to me or even making eye contact. In these schools, everyone was focused on control, as if in anticipation of an imminent "prison riot." Often when I reported for duty in the morning, I would be given the keys to my room and a reminder: "Don't let them out of the room."

Immersed each day in such a culture of fear, teachers locked their doors and kept anything that might be perceived as a chink in their "professional" armor tightly guarded. The unspoken rule among teachers was to never let on that you might not be good at "controlling" your class or that you needed help with anything. Parents were also intimidated by the lock-down culture they encountered at their children's school. Parents were not even allowed to enter some schools without an appointment. Unfortunately, there are schools in which this level of disrespect and fear is the norm, especially in those in which 90 percent or more of the students live below the poverty line.

I couldn't help but compare the intellectually anemic and condescending school settings in Chicago's "inner city" schools to the nurturing, intellectually stimulating education I had received in my small private school and which I knew existed in wealthier suburbs and at Shoesmith. How could a presumed democracy endure, I wondered, while perpetuating a system in which children spend thirteen years in such radically different educational settings depending entirely on their family's income, race, and status?

I was certainly aware of systemic inequality, but I had never experienced firsthand the race- and class-based disparities so concretely displayed as in the schools on Chicago's South Side and the ways they affected children, parents, and teachers. In these schools that prioritized exercising control over building community, students often feared their peers and their teachers, teachers feared their principal, and the fear between families and staff tended to be mutual. In a hierarchical system built on disrespect, the shared understanding was that those "below" one in status didn't deserve the power or respect afforded one's "superiors."

My experience with these disparities also made me aware of another problematic contrast. Ironically, the progressive schools founded in the early part of the last century, including those influenced by the work and philosophy of Maria Montessori, Rudolph Steiner, and John Dewey, which were founded with the vision of serving the children of the working poor, no longer served them. Ethical Culture Fieldston School annually celebrated its founding father's dream of providing working people, mostly immigrants, with an education that would enable them to create a more equal and cooperative world. Yet it has been a long time since ECFS served the community for which it was founded. And, sadly, the humanist values and progressive pedagogy underlying these models never made their mark on public schooling in low-income districts. These ideas have remained primarily rooted in the realm of private education, accessible to an elite minority and explicitly deemed inappropriate for poor children, and, above all, poor children of color.

DISCOVERING WHAT'S POSSIBLE

After subbing for a year, I accepted a half-day kindergarten position at Shoesmith School. Even if teaching five-year-olds was not an inspiring thought at that time, I initially accepted the position because it paid as well as being a substitute and I would no longer have to travel from school to school. But soon after starting my work at Shoesmith, something strange happened to me. I was falling in love! Both with being a teacher and with being part of *a community called school.*

Aside from its diversity, Shoesmith had an unusual faculty of highly educated local women, many of whom were fellow activists. The principal was a young man who aspired to be a high school principal and had no intention of learning a lot about K–6 students. Still, he saw his job as empowering those experienced women to tell him what needed to be done to support their teaching and passing on an encouraging word whenever he could. After my experience of being infantilized by my mostly male school administrators, it was a revelation to me what a difference it made when professionals were provided with autonomy and respect.

Meanwhile, inside my kindergarten classroom, every stereotype that I knew about "those children" and their families was demonstrably dispelled once again. The youngsters—all thirty—and their families were articulate, interesting, and responsive to learning in a progressive classroom. Additionally, Shoesmith's small size allowed everyone to get to know one other—children and adults—and one another's classrooms well. It was an interesting place to be—for everyone.[4] Our days had a fun, productive bustle to them, and because Shoesmith was truly a neighborhood school, I ran into children and families in the course of my daily life outside the school (an aspect of civic life that may well seem quaint in this era of school choice).

Everything about my experience at Shoesmith stimulated me intellectually, morally, socially, and emotionally. I still have the wonderful stories that the children dictated to me and that I turned into small books for them. I still recollect the trips we took, the imaginary cities we invented, and the make-believe stories we told. And I also still remember how the staff initiated me into the habit of "creative noncompliance"—how to avoid complying with district demands when they interfered with our ability to respond to the actual needs and interests of the children in our care. For example, I remember that the district expected all kindergarten teachers to teach the same curriculum. I was particularly mystified by one of the units, which dictated that all Chicago five-year-olds should learn about Los Angeles and Tokyo. I found these choices random and bizarre, and exercised my (albeit fledging) professional judgment to modify the plan: instead of Los Angeles, we studied *Chicago* and Tokyo. For our study of Chicago, I had to design the curriculum myself, so I took the children on lots of trips around the city to study different neighborhoods, the city's public transportation system, and the architecture. Though a study of Tokyo was part of the district plan, I didn't follow that curriculum either. Instead, I had the children wear traditional Japanese clothing and remove their shoes to enter the room. We sat on pillows on the floor and drank from tea cups.

One day a monitor from the Chicago Central District office came, unannounced, to see what I was doing in my first year as a teacher. When she entered the room, she looked very alarmed and asked me to step out in the hall, where she informed me that I was supposed to be studying Tokyo and *Los Angeles*, not Chicago. She also told me that the curriculum was supposed to be emphasizing something or another—I no longer remember. In any case, I argued with her, defending my decisions. She left after reprimanding me and telling me I needed to stop studying Chicago and follow the curriculum content and pacing guide.

My Shoesmith colleagues who had overheard our argument later explained to me that it wasn't safe to argue with the folks from "downtown," that you could lose your job just for making your own decisions about how to run your classroom. Instead, they insisted, I should always apologize, say I didn't know, that of course I'd now be happy to comply and then they'd go away satisfied. It upset me that teachers and principals had to work under conditions that essentially required us to be dishonest with state and district administrators in order to maintain the integrity of our work with children. But it was useful advice, nevertheless—advice I found myself heeding for many years to come.

Despite becoming aware of this disheartening disconnect between education bureaucrats and practitioners, I nevertheless found myself learning every day, from my colleagues, from my young students, and from their families. Even the exercise of having to modify (or replace!) the district curriculum to make it suitable for my students, as well as other challenges such as thinking about how to break down barriers that clearly still existed, even in a conscientious school like Shoesmith (and were all the more visible in my diverse classroom) between the mostly white, middle-class staff and families from different backgrounds, pushed me intellectually and made me a better educator.

And so, for the first time, and without realizing it, I began to take both my role as teacher and as colleague more seriously than my role as amateur sociologist. Even as I dove deeply into these new roles, however, I never stopped thinking of the big picture. My year subbing on Chicago's South Side gave me a good dose of reality regarding the entrenched nature of inequity so visibly manifested in our system of schooling. By contrast, my year teaching kindergarten at Shoesmith helped me understand what *could be* done to make those thirteen years of compulsory schooling a preparation for the kind of active citizenship democracy rests on. What would it take to make public schools look less like factories or prisons and more like Shoesmith? Granted, K–12 students and teachers couldn't make the "revolution" that many of us engaged in the civil rights movement of the early 1960s were beginning to imagine was possible. But, I thought, perhaps schools could become the ground in which the seeds of change were planted.

HOTHOUSING DEMOCRACY

I would have been happy to teach kindergarten at Shoesmith indefinitely, but my husband's work took us to Philadelphia in 1965, where I taught in the first Head Start program as part of President Johnson's War on Poverty. Four-year-olds, it turned out, were as interesting as five-year-olds. The following year we moved to Manhattan, where I surprised my mother and others close to me by taking on another morning kindergarten teaching position, this time at PS 144 in Central Harlem.

During the next few years, four significant things happened that would greatly influence my future ideas about what constituted a democratic school—and why such schools were so important. First, together with three other early childhood teachers, the pre-K teacher, and two first- and second-grade colleagues, and with the support of the principal, we created a "mini-school" within a school at PS 144. My mini-school colleagues and I collaborated closely on just about everything. We had a taste of what it might be like to have the kind of collegial support and professional autonomy many public school teachers only dream about.

Second, shortly after I began teaching at PS 144, I met and began working with an extraordinary educator named Lillian Weber, who would become one of my lifelong mentors. Lillian was deeply influenced by the English infant schools, which would come to be known in the United States as the Open Classroom movement, and in the 1960s established the Workshop Center for Open Education at New York's City College, where she taught in the School of Education. She started a novel project during her time at the Workshop Center, placing volunteer teachers and her student teachers from City College together on one corridor of their school to explore open education practices together. Called the Open Corridor Project, it was an effort to demonstrate the power of collegiality, for teachers and students to learn from one another. Soon after she and I met, Lillian helped us at our PS 144 "mini-school," bringing her student teachers to observe and participate in our work. In 1972, I left PS 144 and began working with Lillian's Workshop Center full time, coaching public school teachers who were interested in creating Open Corridors in their schools.

My third experience occurred during this same period. In the midst of a very divisive and protracted teachers strike that took place during the first half of the 1968–1969 school year, many teachers I knew started what we called "Freedom Schools"—alternative learning sites in their homes, museums, parks, and churches for interested families and students. Four teachers from IS 44, the middle school that my daughter Becky attended across the street from where we lived, asked if they could "hold class" at our home, and we gladly turned our brownstone into a Freedom School. Meanwhile, I too met my students and their families at a nearby Harlem church and then walked to explore Central Park or take the bus to visit local museums.

In addition to giving teachers the liberty to teach an almost entirely experiential curriculum, Freedom Schools also broke down many of the social barriers that had been so entrenched during my time at Shoesmith and ever since. Students and teachers interacted in a much more informal way than they did in their actual classroom settings. The IS 44 staff who met at my place were very happy with this novel way of starting school. Getting to know students and many families in a less rigid setting led us all to form much more collegial and trusting relationships that lasted even after returning to our regular classrooms.

The fourth experience also grew directly out of the Freedom School period. The four IS 44 middle school teachers who had held classes at my house during the strike began discussing the troubling segregation they saw taking place within their school. I was already aware of this problem because my daughter Becky was having a terrible sixth-grade year there. The student body was about 80 percent Black and Latino, with all the white students tracked into "advanced placement" classes. It seemed that the only interactions that Becky had with students of color were physically and verbally threatening clashes in the halls and stairwells.

What began as informal venting sessions among a handful of teachers and parents evolved into more formal planning sessions for how to address the problem, and that soon included input and buy-in from more concerned parents. We came up with a plan to open a small, integrated school-within-a-school pilot program at IS 44. The first task was pushing out a principal who spent most of his time locked away in his office avoiding conflict and for whom teachers, parents, and kids had lost all respect. When I spoke with him about the violence that was occurring in the stairwells, his only advice was to suggest that my child belonged in a better school. This principal retired, however, and was replaced with a man named Luther Seabrook, who made swift and significant changes to the school's culture and tone. With support from Seabrook, the staff, and a group of parents, we created a heterogeneous "school" that would be more or less evenly mixed Black, Latino, and white and fully integrated across ability levels.

The pilot was organized so that just four teachers could plan and teach all academic subjects as a team. In addition to academics, the teachers were very deliberate about creating opportunities for students and families to get to know one another and to form strong ties. I was grateful to be able to send all three of my kids to the pilot and that they were able to develop lasting friendships with such a diverse peer group. Most importantly, I saw that the pilot served as an example within the larger school setting of the power that a small intentional community had to begin to break down race, class, and other barriers.

Common to all four experiences were size (very small), autonomy (we were really on our own), close connections with families, lots of flexibility, and, in most cases, the inclusion of students of varied ages. Maybe, I thought, these were elements that would work in most settings. No doubt there were many other experiences along the way that led me to begin dreaming about starting a small school that did away with traditional hierarchical structures in favor of more democratic structures and relationships. But these were the experiences from which I found myself drawing both inspiration and practical lessons when my colleagues and I eventually *did* get a chance to start our dream school.

That chance came when a new young superintendent in East Harlem's District 4 approached me with a startling offer I couldn't refuse: to start a K–6 school with virtually complete autonomy. So, in the spring of 1974, I gathered like-minded colleagues, many of whom had also worked with Lillian Weber, to help start Central Park East (CPE) as a progressive, staff-governed public elementary school in East Harlem. Committed to the idea of establishing a truly democratic professional environment, we allowed the *why*, *what*, and *how* of the school to emerge from the experiences each of us brought to our work. Not surprisingly, all four of the elements described above were on our collective list.

CPE was one of the first schools to open as part of District 4's Alternative School network, a bold experiment that would eventually result in over thirty small, autonomous schools of choice blossoming throughout one of the city's most troubled and neglected communities. Because all the District 4 alternative schools operated within the regular public school system, we had to navigate the same labor and management requirements as any other public school. But we had enough autonomy over our planning process so that we were able to institute several structures that aligned with our shared interest in John Dewey's philosophy and Jean Piaget's theories of human development, as well as our shared experience working with Lillian Weber.

The staff decided, for example, that mixed-age groupings was something we wanted. We agreed that a class of mixed ages supported diverse ability groupings and allowed teachers to stay with students and families for more than one year, which would help staff build strong relationships with children and families. It also supported another decision we made: to not turn or send away students who might be designated as in need of "special" education. We were, at first, especially appealing to the families of such children. So we explored many structures and practices over the years to accommodate students with special needs, some of which even led the central office to initiate what came to be known as "resource rooms." Throughout each school year, CPE staff made collective decisions about structures, practices, and plans that we felt needed to be tweaked, changed, eliminated, or added in order to meet the needs of a school community that we hoped would coalesce around a shared sense of ownership.

As it turned out, understanding how to share ownership with families was one of the big issues we struggled with during CPE's first years. Quite honestly, I don't think we were aware there was a problem until the parents themselves let us know we were not doing enough to include them, and even then, it took us some time to hear them. I think we believed that, since we were generally more respectful of students and offered them more choice than they would have had in traditional schools, parents would be satisfied. But within the first three years, groups of parents expressed, in one way or another, disappointment over how "teacher focused" the school was, considering our intentional focus on cultivating a democratic community. Parents let us know, some more stridently than others, that they thought they would have more voice in important matters, especially in the curriculum. We replied that ours was an emergent curriculum that the students and teachers were creating based on what was happening in the world and in our community, and on what sparked students' interests.

By year three, CPE even had had a crisis in which one group of parents was so angry they issued an ultimatum to the staff—either I go or they would remove their students, en masse. The District 4 Alternative School manager, Sy Fleigel, stepped in and mediated for us. In the end, only three parents took their children out of the school. But the incident shook us and perhaps woke us up. I think we finally understood how impatient we often were with families. We were so excited (and I guess a bit territorial) about what we saw as *our* dream school project that we tended not to hear what families had to say and would respond defensively.

After our small crisis had passed, CPE staff agreed that we needed help thinking about how to better include families. In year four, we worked with the Ackerman Institute of Family Therapy, which had many years of experience trying to get schools to listen to and hear family voices. They observed us for several months and reviewed our practices, which led to some incredibly helpful recommendations, many of which we ended up incorporating. Some were simple tweaks to our daily routines. For example, they suggested always responding with some version of "I'm so glad you called" whenever a parent phoned the school. The primary purpose of this greeting was not necessarily to make the parent feel better (though that was an important side effect). Rather, the idea was to remind *ourselves* that we should truly be glad that parents were reaching out to us, regardless of the purpose of their call or the tone of their voice. The fact was, any communication was vital, informative, and far better than silence.

Other recommendations from the Ackerman Institute led us to dramatically change certain practices for the better. For example, for the first several years, our family conferences were very traditional, with teachers "telling" families about their children's classwork. The Ackerman Institute observers suggested that we include students in these conferences and leave time and space for everyone to share knowledge and ask questions.

Even as we grappled with these and other questions at CPE 1, around year five, we also began to hit our stride. We had all our grades, K–6, and we had a strong and unusually stable staff who enjoyed working together. We soon had a waiting list of families who wanted their children to attend our school, and our colleagues helped open and introduce similar practices in two new District 4 elementary schools—Central Park East II, in 1981, and River East a few years later. The three schools operated for many years as a close-knit unit—the staff of each negotiating budgets together, agreeing on some basic principles and procedures, and participating in joint work retreats.

In 1984, with the support of education-reform leader Ted Sizer and his newly formed Coalition of Essential Schools, I moved on from my role as director of CPE I to start a high school, Central Park East Secondary School (CPESS) for seventh to twelfth graders. Approximately half of the secondary school student population was drawn from the three CPE elementary schools, and the other half came from other District 4 elementary schools and other neighborhoods, especially central Harlem and Washington Heights, just north of Harlem.

Even as we expanded and grew better at sharing ownership, there were always difficult issues that we continued to explore. One was the ongoing question of who should be included in important decision making: Students? Families? Staff? Community members? Others? What we mean when we say "these schools belong to you and me" is a puzzle that I am still grappling with to this day. But it is a dilemma worth wrestling with in schools, as in our democracy at large.

Another challenge we faced was how to develop practices that would help staff members to take an honest and critical stance toward one another's work. In our experience with the secondary school (CPESS), we had the advantage of being able to learn from CPE. We made clear from the start that since we were all involved in hiring, we all had to be involved in supervising and evaluating our colleagues. Perhaps one of the most powerful structures we established at CPESS was student advisories. Each staff member met daily for about an hour with the same group of students, if possible over the course of two years. It was in advisories that students could talk about what was happening at home, in their social lives, discuss books they were reading, and write in their journals. It was also a time when advisors raised issues related to sex and health education and discussed college preparation, possibilities for the future summer plans, and much more. In other words, advisory was a social and academic support group for students, and it was also a way for staff to build strong relationships with students. And in cultivating trusting relationships with kids, advisories also allowed staff to build strong relationships and channels of communication with families.

All of these various experiences together led to the development of practices and convictions that I thought worthy of attempting to bring to scale in New York City and taking with me two decades later when I started Mission Hill School with a team of talented friends and educators in Boston. What stood out most to me, however, was the impact on all of us in all these varied experiences of being in a community that was concerned with educating for democracy by educating *as* a democracy.

CHAPTER 4

REINVIGORATING THE COMMONWEAL

THE MISSION HILL SCHOOL EXAMPLE

Emily Gasoi

> Good schools focus on habits, on what sort of intellectual activities will and should inform their graduates' lives. Not being clear . . . leads to mindlessness . . . to drifting along doing what we do simply because we have always done it that way. Such places are full of silly compromises, of practices that boggle commonsense analysis. . . . The purpose of education is not in keeping school but in pushing out into the world young citizens who are soaked in habits of thoughtfulness and reflectiveness, joy, and commitment.
>
> —TED SIZER in *Horace's School*[1]

MANY OF THE QUESTIONS that arose in those first formative years at Mission Hill School were practical in nature, from how to organize lunch and dismissal patterns to how successful we were at integrating math into the project-based curriculum. The slew of practical and pressing questions often needed to be addressed *yesterday*. Every new school has its fires to extinguish, but as teachers in a staff-governed school, it felt like a windblown brush fire that we confronted on a daily basis. For the MHS staff, it began on the first day of school when the furniture we ordered still hadn't arrived. We pooled our resources and brought in mismatched chairs, tables of varied shapes and sizes, rugs and pillows for our meeting areas and library corners, baskets to serve as bookshelves, and so on. When the students arrived, they found a homey-looking school that ended up satisfying our attempts to create a family feel better than if we had started off with our scholastic furnishings. Most of us ended up keeping elements of our homespun classrooms, even after our scholastic furniture arrived.

Most of the fires to which we had to attend, however, were not so easily addressed, as when Angel, our fourth-fifth grade teacher left us before winter break. As a close-knit staff, losing Angel was a blow to our morale. Throughout our collective soul-searching over losing a valuable member of our team, we had to move quickly to find a strong colleague and teacher to take over Angel's classroom. In a democratically governed school, filling these positions as quickly (yesterday) but also as thoughtfully (we had to find candidates who understood and embraced the fundamentals of progressive pedagogy) as possible fell not just to the administration but to the entire staff. We had to rapidly assemble a hiring committee and figure out a schedule for covering one another's classrooms while some of us participated in the interview process. We then spent much of our staff meeting time considering the recommendations of the hiring committee before collectively choosing our new colleagues.

Some problems were beyond our control, such as when, during the first winter, the radiators in the hundred-year-old Jesuit high school building we had moved into malfunctioned, counterintuitively turning the north side of the building into a burning desert and the south side into an Arctic tundra. Other problems we were able to quell relatively quickly. When it surfaced that an academically advanced third grader was quietly bullying his peers, the staff decided to convene a student lunch group, made up of students identified as both bullies and victims, that would meet to discuss the impact of and possible solutions for the bullying problem. The staff also agreed that the student in question was socially sophisticated enough and academically prepared to move to an older classroom where he was less likely to be in a position to intimidate his peers.

Still, some fires smoldered and sprang up repeatedly over the years: there were always families who complained that there was not enough homework, while others claimed there was too much; some argued that the homework required too much family involvement, while others conveyed to us how much they appreciated the family component. In fact, the staff had hotly debated whether or not to have homework. There was general agreement among us that children learned at least as much at home as they did at school. We had them for over six hours a day; why should our agenda reach into their family time as well? The compromise we came up with was to give homework tasks that we felt would ignite students' intrinsic sense of curiosity and that would invite family participation. For example, in the fall, second and third graders might be asked to find an array of different colored leaves and to come up with a hypothesis as to why they changed. A fourth-fifth-grade classroom might be asked to choose a family member to interview about a particular area of expertise or a school-related topic.

Of course, the needs that felt most immediate were the everyday human dramas and ongoing academic dilemmas that played out in our school community: when my father died two weeks into our first school year; when a third grader who had become uncharacteristically lethargic in school finally revealed that his father had been incarcerated the week before; when a teacher noticed that an articulate, intellectually sharp fourth grader who loved telling long, intricate stories could not read above a first-grade level; when a group of K–1 girls were found to be systematically excluding other children from their play.

Admittedly, the responsibility the staff had for developing every aspect of the school's culture and practices sometimes felt overwhelming. And given the extra hours we put into meeting, developing curricula and assessments, among other responsibilities, these strong collegial connections felt essential. On an emotional level, it was important that I actually looked forward to spending that extra time with my colleagues. On a practical level, the fact that we regularly shared how we were approaching curriculum and lesson planning, discussed breakthroughs and challenges we were experiencing, and various questions that invariably arose about students, our practice, families, or a myriad other classroom issues made it easier to act as informed allies and resources to one another in matters both great and small. If I needed more sugar cubes for students who were working on a model of an ancient Mayan pyramid, I could send them to ask Heidi, whom I knew was working on a similar project, to lend us some. If Geralyn needed an older student to help calm down one of her first graders or assist a group of kindergarten students complete a task, I knew which of my students would be best for the job. When I needed to address an emotionally charged topic with a parent (as when a mother came in to challenge my decision to hang a poster of famous gay and lesbian writers in our classroom), I knew I could call on any one of my colleagues to step in for a few moments while I gathered my thoughts.

Precisely because there were always pressing matters and emergencies, big and small, it was imperative that the whole staff be able to assemble often and communicate with ease. In turn, productive communication depended on developing trusting relationships and a strong sense of shared responsibility for the school. In the small private school where I had previously worked, I had known all my colleagues, but still, that school was not as small as MHS, where, for many years, the staff could all fit around one table. At MHS, I was acutely aware of my colleagues' work. I knew their students, their struggles and triumphs. As a result, I felt deeply invested in our collective success. Of course, there were disagreements and difficulties, but overall, there was an incredible sense of empowerment in our collaboration.

COLLECTIVE CURRICULUM AS INTELLECTUAL WELLSPRING

Early December 1997, we were wrapping up our first three-month "Near and Dear" study exploring the community around the school, and our very first family night was fast approaching. Students were putting finishing touches on their projects, practicing their presentations, studying their "docent" cheat sheets so they'd be able to explain their own and their classmates' work to family members without consulting their notes. Students in my second-third-grade classroom had decided to do a study of the MHS neighborhood's unique geological features—the school was situated on a high hill with a century-old puddingstone quarry at the end of the street, and there were also outcroppings of puddingstone scattered throughout the area. Our resident curriculum consultant, Joyce Stevens, had learned the history of these rocks and had taken us on an initial tour that included several buildings constructed from the dark-hued stone and an exposed puddingstone shelf that students could climb around and from which they collected samples. Going through my lesson plans and classroom notes from that time, I found an entry in which students had brought the stones back to the classroom for examination. I asked them what they noticed and wrote down their questions and responses.

> "Why is it called *pudding*stone?" seven-year-old Jessamine
> wondered. "Pudding is squishy, but this is hard."
> "I think maybe it used to be squishy," eight-year-old Eli
> suggested.
> "Do you think we might be able to find evidence of that?" I
> asked, encouraging them to use one of our five habits of
> mind—thinking about *how we know what's true and false.*
> "Maybe there is still some of the stones that are more like
> pudding—like maybe they're squishy like Jessamine said,
> and we could look for that?" Serena suggested.
> "Or if we break the rocks up, maybe there would be pudding
> inside?" another student ventured.

I pointed out that a clue might be another name we had learned, *conglomerate stone.* I sent a few students to look it up in the dictionary, and then I continued our discussion, questioning students about what they had noticed, wondered, and surmised about puddingstone.

The Mission Hill neighborhood is part of the Roxbury section of Boston, and so one day a student asked if the name *Roxbury* had anything to do with the special rocks we were learning about. I secretly thought this was a silly question, but I kept my best teacher face and encouraged the student to add it to the list of ongoing questions we had hanging on one of the bulletin boards dedicated to our study. As it turned out, however, this student proved that no query is unworthy, as we learned from a visiting geologist from the Massachusetts Institute of Technology that Roxbury had indeed originally been called *Rocksbury.* The students began to talk about names of other Boston neighborhoods, exercising the habit of mind *connections: is there a pattern?* Some, such as neighboring Dorchester, where many of our students lived, took their names from old English towns; others, such as Mattapan, were mispronunciations of indigenous names; and Mission Hill was named for the grand cathedral that stood majestically at the bottom of the hill and was built from, yes, you guessed it, Roxbury puddingstone.

The conversation continued not just over the course of that day but throughout the three months of the schoolwide "Near and Dear" study. Over time, however, students' questions and ideas became increasingly more informed as we gathered information from geology books, guest experts, visits to the science museums, and to nearby Fitzgerald Park, built on puddingstone.

While the study of the Mission Hill neighborhood was a schoolwide endeavor, each classroom began with a different focus. Alicia's K–1 classroom focused on local businesses and then chose one to emulate, opening a bakery in their classroom, while Geralyn's K–1 class studied local architecture but eventually became obsessed with snails they found in abundance in the school yard. Heidi's second-third-grade classroom decided to study the history of the neighborhood's changing demographics throughout the twentieth century by interviewing longtime residents, including several inhabitants of the local senior home. Angel's fourth-fifth graders didn't follow the theme, except when one group of girls' interest in dollhouses happened to overlap with the architecture study that Geralyn's class was doing.

As our respective neighborhood studies evolved over the first several weeks, they began to overlap and intertwine. In part this was probably because we frequently met together as a staff to discuss our progress, share ideas and resources, and problem solve. In so doing, we invariably spread common ideas across our classrooms. We also all used the Habits of Mind to guide our work, and that too created continuity among classrooms. But there also seemed to be an organic quality to the cross-pollination of ideas. Students from each class shared work-in-progress during our weekly Friday assemblies and then informally as our work spilled out into the long, wide hallway that ran from one end of the school to the other, connecting all the classrooms. Students and teachers stopped to watch and interact with their schoolmates and colleagues at work constructing, writing explanations and reports, and drawing diagrams and informative posters. As a result, students became interested in the work they saw going on in other classrooms.

Soon, kids in my class were taking interested groups of younger and older students on tours of the puddingstone quarry at the end of the street, and students in our sister second-third-grade classroom were acting as ambassadors for other students interested in visiting residents at the senior home. The oldest students had inspired the younger kids to recreate some of the neighborhood monuments in the block area, including the Mission Hill Cathedral, the library, students' homes, and the school itself. There was also an easy marriage between the puddingstone and architecture studies, as we learned that many of the most prominent buildings in the neighborhood and beyond were built with it. And snails, of all things, became a schoolwide obsession. In fact, when a newspaper reporter called in mid-October to interview Deb and asked what we were studying, the first thing that came out of her mouth was "Snails."

And so, by the time the first family night rolled around, most of the classrooms had terrariums filled with snails, accompanied by scientific drawings and written pieces about the lives of snails; students of all ages had built models of various neighborhood structures, which they constructed using an assortment of materials, including papier maché, cardboard and found objects, and blocks; students from both second-third-grade classrooms teamed up to create a topographical map of the terrain for one square block surrounding the school based on the geological research they ended up doing together; and a group of fourth-fifth graders had joined the younger students in interviewing seniors, and the mixed-age team wrote and performed skits based on the stories they recorded. Some students presented their individual work, while others teamed up to complete a project and then took turns explaining their work to families, who circulated through the five classrooms.

The months leading up to this culminating family night felt hectic, even overwhelming at times. Keeping up with students' interests, supplying them with the materials they needed to tinker, experiment, and construct the projects they devised to convey their ideas and knowledge, left us adults somewhat breathless at times. But we were able to share resources, and the enthusiasm we saw students express for their own and one another's work, within and across classrooms, was thrilling. We were all energized by the percolation of ideas that was animating our new school, bringing to life our collective works-in-progress. And though much of the sharing of interests and ideas that took place during our schoolwide theme work felt organic, such collaboration was sparked and sustained within the structures that Deb, building on decades of experience, had very deliberately introduced when starting the school. Once the structures were established, she handed the reigns to the staff.

TESTING VALUES

What the MHS staff did not know in 1997 was that we were establishing our new pilot school on what would turn out to be a political fault line between state and district reform policies. At the district level, Boston schools superintendent, Thomas Payzant, in partnership with the Boston Teachers Union and local school leaders, was in the midst of enacting a system-wide initiative to entrust principals and teachers with more autonomy through the Pilot School initiative. In order to offset competition that a recently passed law allowing charter schools to open throughout the state portended, Boston Public Schools invested pilots with charter-like autonomy to innovate, including control over their budgets, staffing decisions, and program design. In addition to these autonomies, pilot school leaders successfully advocated for the right to develop alternative forms of student assessment and accountability systems in place of the standardized tests. However, only a year after MHS opened its doors, the Commonwealth of Massachusetts unfurled one of the most stringent, high-stakes accountability systems in the country.

While Boston went forward with its progressive pilot initiative, in the larger state arena it began to rain sticks and carrots. Sticks came in the form of threats of sanctions that would be used to "fix" schools whose students scored poorly on the state's standardized tests, the Massachusetts Comprehensive Assessment System (MCAS). Sanctions—beyond the pillory of printing schools' low scores in public forums—included threats of measures such as cuts to funding, reconstitution of staff, and transfer of governance to state or private oversight. Carrots arrived in the form of rewards such as public praise and increased funding.

These changes were the beginning manifestations of a seven-year plan put in motion by the 1993 Massachusetts Education Reform

Act. As is often the case, Massachusetts's education policy fore-shadowed what would soon become a national trend. While a shift toward market-infused education reform was taking shape across the country, Massachusetts was the first state to actualize a plan based in the business community's understanding of the best way forward for public education. The Reform Act closely followed the agenda advanced in a 1991 Massachusetts Business Alliance for Education report entitled *Every Child a Winner!* Written just as the state was emerging from a period of fiscal decline and poised at the gates of the new millennium, the MBAE report strikes an urgent tone, warning that public education in Massachusetts was in a state of crisis that warranted immediate and dramatic reform.

The report identified the need for the state to overhaul an in-herently inequitable funding structure and a generally outmoded education system that was "failing to provide its students with the knowledge and skills necessary for them to be productive, informed citizens in coming decades."[2] Based on this assessment, MBAE called for the state to create a more equitable funding structure while holding schools more accountable for meeting their respon-sibility to students, taxpayers, and, ultimately, the common good. Defining accountability by business standards, however, led to the recommendation of "specific and measurable" goals in the form of uniform state standards and market-oriented consequences for schools that failed to meet the externally defined goals. As the re-port outlines, the state should declare "an unsatisfactory school as 'educationally bankrupt' which would trigger reconstitution of the school and invocation of limited 'choice' or privatization."

The MBAE report became the framework for the 1993 Reform Act. Following the business community's priorities and under-standing of how best to improve schools to meet the known and yet-to-be-understood challenges of twenty-first-century society, the reform plan included a new funding structure that promised a minimum funding allocation to local districts and offered more site-based control for principals in some matters, such as budget and staffing, but within a system that induced them, through incentives and penalties, to follow externally developed standards and meet yearly student achievement benchmarks defined by a measurable bottom line. Thus, several years before the federal No Child Left Behind (NCLB) accountability bill would impose similar mandates nationwide, Massachusetts required all schools to adopt the state standards and for students in grades four, eight, and ten to show proficiency on the newly minted MCAS test, which, it was hoped, would leverage comprehensive school reform outlined in the MBAE report.

Unfortunately, Boston's standardized testing waiver for pilot schools did not protect MHS from state (and, later, federal) mandates. As mentioned above, before the passage of NCLB, in 2001, Massachusetts only mandated testing in grades four, eight, and ten. Mission Hill School started with kindergarten through grade five, adding a grade each year. So, for the first few years after the new state accountability system was enacted, MHS administered the MCAS math and reading tests in grade four without spending any significant school time to teach to the tests. After the second year, however, the staff decided that the school should take an active stance against the testing mandates. Some staff members and families saw the value of using test scores as one more data point in conjunction with several other formal and informal assessment sources that could help us understand more about our students' learning and our practice. But we were unanimous in our objection to the power that the state had vested in MCAS scores to supplant all other measures. Further, the design of the tests and the threat of stringent accountability measures attached to them contradicted many of the staff's fundamental beliefs about the purpose of schooling, what constitutes an effective learning community, and what it means to be educated.

Once No Child Left Behind passed, the state standards and testing extended down to third grade and up through eighth grade. While math and language arts standards tended to focus on broad skills and concepts, the content that students were expected to master for other subject areas was expansive. For example, according to the Massachusetts Department of Education, the scope and sequence of the third-fourth-grade history and social science section of the MCAS requires students to "learn" the following standards-based material over the course of a school year: the history of Massachusetts from the Pilgrims to the present, including the most prominent Massachusetts citizens; the geography and significant physical features of Massachusetts and other northeastern states; important civics topics, including information about local government, prominent local landmarks, and key national documents; and, finally, the relationship between various economic systems and forces, such as business, industry, and taxes.

Though the intention of compelling schools to adopt the state standards in all subjects was to promote equitable school-content offerings and universal competency across subject areas, the material that the state required teachers to "cover" tended to be a mile wide and an inch deep and posed multiple practical and philosophical challenges for our young school. Further, the state subject standards were organized in multi-grade strands but combined differently from MHS's multi-age classrooms. For example, I would have to draw from both the first-second grade and the third-fourth grade curriculum frameworks in order to teach all the material I was expected to cover in my second-third-grade classroom.

There were many benefits to organizing a curriculum as we did that would be lost if we followed grade-specific content standards. Having schoolwide themes allowed students of all ages to approach the same material at very different stages of development, while coming to see one another—but especially their older peers—as "experts" from whom they could learn. Also, we studied the same themes every four years, so students had the opportunity to revisit the same topic at different levels of sophistication, first when they were in kindergarten and again when they were in fourth grade on through eighth grade. This meant that, as a school, we could justify ordering high-quality, sometimes expensive theme-related resources because they would be used by so many of us, over and over again.

Finally, Mission Hill School's theme-based curriculum was designed to allow teachers and students to learn basic skills through diving deeply into a small number of broad subject areas. Drawing on the Coalition of Essential Schools' Ten Principles and the MHS's Five Habits of Mind, we took a long view of learning, facilitating projects that helped students develop skills as tools they could use to define and pursue their own interests. We strove to develop a curriculum and a culture that would cultivate what Ted Sizer describes as intellectually "hungry students"[3]—those who are genuinely interested in making sense of the world around them, who are not afraid to tinker, to question, to wrestle with open-ended questions, to get wrong answers, and to make mistakes. These were the skills that we, as teachers modeling democratic practices, felt we needed. And these were also the skills that would serve students, much better than test-taking strategies, as they navigated the then as yet unknown workplace and societal demands of the twenty-first century. While schools like ours were in the minority within the public school system, we felt as if we were on the right side of history.

DEPTH OVER BREADTH IN PRACTICE

Drawing on archived newsletters and old VHS footage of my classroom's 1998 study of ancient Mayan culture, I was struck by a class meeting about a month into our study when the students arrived at a consensus that our culminating project should be to turn our coatroom into a tomb for the ancient Mayan monarch, King Pacal.

"What will we need to find out in order to reconstruct King Pacal's tomb as accurately as possible?" I asked.

Student responses reveal the individual entry points they took into this study, as well as the aspects of ancient civilization with which they were grappling. For example, Jeremy, one of the youngest students in the class, seemed to wrestle with the essential question of what it means to be *ancient* (perhaps sparked by a program we had watched that showed modern-day Mayans exploring ancient ruins in Mexico). He asked, "Are there still ancient Mayan people alive today?" Mishra, a third grader mature beyond his nine years, wanted to know, "Was everyone buried in the same kind of tomb, or were there different kinds of tombs for kings and regular people—you know, like all the workers and stuff?" Linda, a second grader who had taken a particular interest in hieroglyphic writing, responded, "We need to know what they wrote on the outside and around the sides [of the tomb and sarcophagus]."

I remember a moment, perhaps a week prior to this meeting, when Linda lit up during one of our visits to the Ancient Mayan exhibit at Boston's Museum of Fine Arts. She stood with two of her friends, beaming as she pointed to the hieroglyphics carved into a massive sarcophagus lid.

"Look! That one says 'water'!" The three girls sat on the floor in front of the sarcophagus copying a series of glyphs into their class notebooks. When I asked what they were doing, Linda explained that they were each copying a section to decipher once they got back to the classroom so that they could understand more of what was written on the lid.

Over the weeks that followed, students gradually transformed our coatroom into King Pacal's tomb. First, students chose to work independently, in pairs, or in groups, collecting data from books, videos, museum trips, and one another. The next phase included extended visits to the art room to create the contents of the tomb, including the richly adorned skeletal remains of the king and his sarcophagus.

Clearly, this study integrated literature, history, social studies, and art, but how did math figure in this immersion? Students learned the ancient Mayan base-twenty counting system, which involved deciphering symbols, adding, and multiplication. The ancient Mayans were one of the few cultures that developed the idea of zero holding place value, which was another important mathematical concept that students explored. Building King Pacal's tomb also involved quite a bit of mathematical thinking. Students had to figure the dimensions of the coatroom and fashion a sarcophagus that would fit. They had to think about the relative sizes of bones in the body. In fact, two boys working on the skull briefly argued with a group working on the rest of the skeleton because they found the body much too small in relation to the head. In the end, they did some research and were surprised to find out that our ancient Mayan king would have been much smaller than the average modern American adult male. The boys ended up making a new, smaller skull to fit with the proportions of the skeleton.

If we had been forced to follow the overblown scope and sequence of the state standards to prepare students to score well on the MCAS subject tests, it would have been impossible to carry out the kind of in-depth, integrated, and engaging study that is integral to the MHS mission. But as much as MHS teachers objected to the narrowing effect that external standards would have on our curriculum, we also rejected the implicit assumption that all children should learn the same material at the same time. Though staff consulted state standards in designing aspects of school curriculum, the notion that every child in a particular grade could and would learn everything the standards mandated within a specified time period was ludicrous. In language arts, MHS took the stance that pressuring students to reach a series of literacy benchmarks by a certain age was not only unrealistic but also had the potential to seriously hinder the progress of some students' individual paths to becoming literate.

Another example from my classroom highlights the importance of respecting students' individual learning processes. Christina was a bilingual student whose parents had emigrated from Puerto Rico when she was an infant. She lived in subsidized housing in Roxbury and had attended a large, overpopulated school before coming to MHS. When she graduated from the eighth grade, Christina was an outgoing, gregarious student who smiled easily, radiating self-confidence and a sense of satisfaction—a remarkable change. Had she remained in her old school, Christina would have been held back in the first grade, her mother explained, because she spent most of her time in class crying in a corner. Christina entered MHS as a second grader, and she did spend the first two weeks or so crying in my classroom as well.

However, at MHS, Christina's transformation manifested most noticeably in her increasing confidence and self-identification as a reader and writer. I cannot pinpoint the precise moment when she gave up her self-imposed exile and became a member of our community. Perhaps it was a combination of daily read-alouds that she could listen to from her corner, a well-stocked and organized classroom library, and the establishment of a safe social environment, among other factors. I first noticed Christina choosing picture books during silent reading time, quietly mouthing words as she turned the pages. During project periods, while other students were building, painting, or acting out skits, Christina continued to pore over picture books. When I felt that I had gained her trust, I asked if she would mind reading me a story. She smiled shyly and nodded. She chose one of her favorites, a beautifully illustrated "Puss in Boots." She then "read" it to me.

Christina did not actually read the words on the page but told her own tale based on the illustrations. Her stories were intricate and detailed. She took visible pleasure in the telling, using varying inflections, gesticulating, and conveying characters' emotions in her facial expressions. I wrote down her stories and she stapled the pages together to make little books. She was able to read her own words more easily than those in the other picture books she loved. She began to dictate her stories to me or to other students in the class on a regular basis and then take them off to read. Eventually her initial shyness abated. She would tell stories with the class during "author share" and received positive feedback from peers. When we then paired students with younger reading partners, Christina would read her own stories or tell stories based on book illustrations.

By spring, Christina was able to read many words in the books she chose from the class library. She began to use her dictated stories as references for writing stories on her own. If Christina had been tested at this point, her scores would have indicated that she was reading "below grade level." If I had viewed her in these terms, my observations would have confirmed this assessment. It was true that Christina was not as strong at decoding text as many other students her age. It was clear that her English vocabulary was still developing, as she sometimes replaced English words with Spanish ones when she spoke. But it was also true that Christina was one of the most *literary* children in the class. That is, despite shortcomings in the mechanics of reading and writing, she was passionate about books, riveted by good literature (as evidenced by her rapt attention when I read aloud to the class), and a gifted storyteller.

Christina devoured picture and chapter books, those that she could read, as well as those beyond her reading level. She regularly opted to join reading groups with students reading at a higher level. I am not sure how old she was when it was determined that she was reading at grade level. It hardly seemed to matter—it was clearly her love of books and stories that drove her to learn the discrete literacy skills involved in reading and writing fluidly.

Beyond school walls, families were bombarded with information about MCAS, including automated phone calls from the mayor's office, and test-prep material being handed out at tollbooths. At MHS, these and other issues related to state mandates were the subject of numerous staff and board meetings. Since the MHS governance board—composed of staff, students, families, and community members—made it an option for families to have their children take the test or not, they wanted to make sure that parents understood what was and *what was not* at stake for their children. For example, though the school and district might be penalized if students scored poorly on the state tests, MHS staff would not base school evaluations or decisions about grade promotion on students' test scores. In fact, there would be no benefits or consequences for students until tenth grade, when their ability to obtain a high school diploma would be based almost exclusively on their performance on the MCAS.

The MHS governing board unanimously agreed that testing in the elementary and middle school grades was not educationally sound. Given our responsibility to do what was best for kids, the staff decided that we would not allow state mandates to change our practices. Mission Hill School wasn't alone in its opposition to the new testing requirements. Other progressive schools in the greater Boston area, such as Fenway High School and the Graham and Parks K–8 school, had a large proportion of their families opting out of the state tests. According to documentation by the National Center for Fair and Open Testing (FairTest), protests against the increasingly high stakes attached to the tests grew, both in numbers and types of schools represented, after the requirement for students to pass the tenth-grade MCAS in order to earn a high school diploma went into effect in 2003. Students, teachers, and families from a wide range of schools, including many traditional public schools, began to publicly articulate their opposition to the new accountability mandates.

A FairTest report describes one city council hearing, for instance, at which more than two hundred constituents spoke against allowing a single test score to outweigh data from other sources, such as grades and other school-based assessments, including human judgment.[4] As one high school student from a Title 1 Boston public school is reported to have testified, "You're pushing out the very students that education reform was supposed to support. . . . You are telling me that because I failed this one test, I can't fulfill my dreams."[5] A teacher from the city's oldest and most prestigious exam school, Boston Latin, led a chant in which he asked, "Whose schools?" and the gathered constituents responded, "Our schools!"

At MHS, the governance board asked the staff to draft a formal statement explaining more directly the school's position on MCAS and gave Deb the authority to inform parents that they had a choice as to whether their child would sit for the test. In 2001, the MHS parent council distributed to parents the following statement drafted by the staff and governance board:

> State-imposed MCAS tests are incompatible with the mission, values and goals of the Mission Hill School and undermine our more rigorous preparation for high school. We believe that the MCAS in its present form will cause harm to students in all schools and to education in Massachusetts. Furthermore, we believe that decisions regarding a student's grades, . . . promotion, and graduation should be made by . . . family and school, [who are] most knowledgeable about the child—and not by a State test score alone.

In lieu of test scores and in accordance with our pilot-school agreement, MHS staff had developed alternative assessments of student achievement and progress. Annually, parents and their children in grades K–5 received two narrative reports, two report cards, and entering and midyear literacy assessments based on audiotaped reading interviews and prompted writing samples. In addition, two teacher-student-family conferences and ongoing student portfolios documented students' progress during their time at MHS.

By the time students reached the sixth grade, the assessment process became more intensive and integrated into the learning process itself. To demonstrate their preparation for high school, middle school students had to undergo a rigorous and reflective process; they prepared portfolios in six subjects over the course of their sixth- to eighth-grade years. Students defended their work before a committee of staff, a peer, one family member, and an external community member in several sessions throughout their eighth-grade year. Community members from a range of backgrounds, including lawyers, entrepreneurs, high school teachers, and university professors, have repeatedly expressed amazement at MHS students' demonstrations of competency in an impressive array of skills, including public speaking, reading and writing in a variety of genres, creating visual displays of their work, and providing impromptu responses to the committee's questions.

It is no accident that MHS's graduation standards place emphasis on presentation as an authentic way for students to demonstrate not only their learning but also their interests, challenges, and discontents. The culture of presenting and sharing is strong in the school; all children, regardless of age, are expected to share finished pieces and works in progress, and to provide and respond to feedback as a matter of course. Students who have spent some time at the school are quite comfortable presenting before audiences of all sorts and sizes because they are accustomed to sharing work and ideas in a variety of settings: during weekly whole-school gatherings, on a daily basis in classrooms, at family conferences where students explain their work to their parents, and during frequent in-class and all-school performances. This practice of sharing and feedback provided teachers with a form of ongoing student assessment and students with the opportunity to practice presentation and communication skills. At bottom, helping students develop their own voice was the intention that guided much of our work. Providing students with as many formal and informal opportunities to practice voicing and defending their ideas, as well as listening and responding to the ideas of others, became the intersection where Dewey's notion of "associative living" met school-based standards and assessment. These ideas are clearly woven together in a passage from the MHS mission statement:

> Our community must be prepared to spend time even when it might seem wasteful hearing each other out. . . . We must expect the most from everyone, hold all to the highest standards, but also

CHAPTER 5

THE FALSE PROMISE OF HIGH-STAKES ACCOUNTABILITY

A CENTURY OF MISUSED METHODS

Deborah Meier

When people vary greatly, as schoolchildren do, and when they are pressed into work they have not chosen, it is foolish to expect them all to meet a set of predetermined standards. Indeed, it is obvious that we do not expect everyone to meet one standard, because we persist in giving tests that rank students into quartiles, quintiles, deciles, and percentiles. . . . Why do we do this, if our objective is to be sure that all students meet a predetermined standard? . . . And what is our reaction when, by some wonderful chance or superb effort, all or most students achieve the standard? Why, of course, we raise it.

—NEL NODDINGS
in *Education and Democracy in the 21st Century*[1]

I DIDN'T ALWAYS have negative feelings about testing. I believed that tests were scientific, objective in a way that classroom teachers couldn't be. I never took a standardized test during my years at my progressive, private school. The first standardized tests I remember taking were in college. I had to take an entrance exam to get into the University of Chicago graduate school to study history. I did very well on the exam, even though I had done nothing to prepare for it and knew almost nothing about the subject matter. My future husband, Fred Meier, who never graduated from high school for a mix of complicated reasons, also tested into this same prestigious university. I was thus happy to embrace the commonly held belief that standardized tests could prove scientifically that we were both very smart. I saw that the tests we took made it possible for us to prove our intelligence to the college admissions board regardless of our family's different class backgrounds.

Over time, however, I came to suspect tests were not as valid or reliable a marker of intelligence as I had once believed. As a parent, I experienced a dramatic disconnect between what I knew about my children's abilities and what their test scores seemed to indicate. The first challenge involved my son, Nicky. A few months after he started third grade at our neighborhood public school in upper Manhattan, Nicky's teacher informed me that he needed remedial reading instruction based on the results of the standardized reading test for his grade. I was startled. I assumed tests would reveal that our children had inherited their parents' "native intelligence." What made these results particularly baffling, however, was the dissonance between what the test results seemed to "objectively" reveal about Nicky's reading ability and my own knowledge of him as a reader. Nicky was one of those early fluent and sophisticated readers, devouring books at home faster than we could provide new ones. This incongruity led me to investigate just what had happened to make Nicky score so badly. I found a copy of an old third-grade reading test, which wasn't hard to do in those days, and administered it to my son.

Right away I noticed Nicky doing something unusual: upon completing a reading passage, he covered it with his hand before attempting to respond to the set of related questions in the test booklet. When I asked him about this strategy, Nicky proceeded to reveal a line of reasoning that I am certain the test makers had not anticipated. He insisted that it was "only fair" because it would be "cheating" to look back at them. I explained he didn't need to do this—in fact, that he definitely *should not* do so. But he argued that if he could keep looking back at the reading passages to inform his answers, it wouldn't be a good measure of his understanding. I also saw that he wrote little notes next to some of the possible responses explaining why he thought C was the "right" answer, even though he suspected the author of the test thought it should be D. Fortunately I convinced him (though not easily) not to use these overly conscientious strategies on future tests, even though, at that young age, he seemed to have developed a moral objection to adopting more traditional tactics.

Having uncovered the cause of my son's misleading test results, I tried to present evidence to Nicky's teacher that he was, in fact, a strong reader. To my surprise and increasing disbelief, it seemed that no evidence beyond the test would alter her opinion. Nicky should have remedial instruction, she insisted. Fortunately, the principal agreed that if I didn't want him to get special help, he wouldn't have to.[2] Needless to say, after some coaching from me, Nicky scored well on the spring reading test. These results greatly pleased his teacher, and the next time we saw one another, she pointed out that we had "worked well together" at helping him "improve." I thought, "You must be joking!" But I held my tongue. I was learning to choose my battles.

A few months later, I began teaching kindergarten at PS 144 in Central Harlem, and the extent to which tests misrepresented students' actual abilities began to appear ubiquitous. But since I taught kindergarten, I didn't yet have any firsthand experience with citywide testing, and I still believed in their basic objectivity and usefulness; I assumed that Nicky's problems had to do primarily with his own particular quirks and not with the tests themselves. It didn't occur to me at that time to consider that most kids have their own "particular quirks" and that Nicky was surely not the only child to have his own ideas about how to approach the test and how to interpret the questions. And, of course, not all parents in the same situation would feel they were in a position to challenge test scores that countered their own knowledge of their child's abilities.

It was during my third year at PS 144 that three of my colleagues and I convinced the principal to transform the early childhood wing of the school into a "mini-school" comprising prekindergarten through second grade. We were especially excited at the prospect of being able to work as a team with students as they moved through the grades. The reading test was given in second grade, and we thought we would be able to see the progress kids made in reading as a result of their time in our "mini-school." At the time, the second-grade tests were not "high stakes" in the sense they are today, but they surely had an impact on how parents and teachers viewed a child's learning abilities, as well as on how the children felt about themselves. Student test scores also had some impact on how parents and principals perceived the competence of particular teachers and, even then, probably influenced how much a teacher might focus on test prep.

My mini-school colleagues and I had high expectations for our young charges. Unfortunately, when our first group of second graders took the test, their scores were not as strong as we had hoped they might be. Our administration wasn't particularly concerned with the results because the scores were on par with the city and schoolwide grade-two scores, and these second graders had only been in our mini-school for less than a year. What my team found unsettling, however, was that the results indicated that several youngsters who we *knew* were very strong and avid readers had scored as "nonreaders" on the test!

It was during this period that I began to spend my free time researching the historical and contemporary practices regarding test development and use. What I discovered brought to light what at best could be considered a flawed instrument, and at worst, a mechanism for maintaining the so-called achievement gap that test proponents claim they are being used to close. During that year, I received a small grant to do more research on standardized testing and to write about my findings. As part of this work, my colleagues and I began to interview children, individually and in small groups, to better understand the reasoning they used when responding to questions on the reading test.[3] As we discussed their way of thinking about a specific question, as well as their general approach to taking the test, we found that each student was able to provide a logical rationale. I began to have a sense of déjà vu, as their responses were similar to what my son's had been—perceiving the test questions from an angle my colleagues and I would never have thought of. Only, unlike Nicky, our students didn't seem to distinguish between what they thought was right and what they believed the test makers would want them to circle. They were simply interpreting the items and the answers differently—I thought quite sensibly, which often caused me to doubt my own preferred answers to the second-grade reading test.

In 1972, I began publishing essays and speaking out against the overuse and misuse of standardized tests, which, I argued, did more to confirm students' economic status than to provide any useful data on reading ability. I wish I could say that my fellow testing detractors and I were successful in convincing stakeholders and policymakers to pursue more sound forms of accountability, that nothing more needs to be written on the issue. Unfortunately, testing has been a perennial battle that my colleagues and I continue to fight, now more vigorously than ever as they are now used for more and more high-stakes purposes (and the individual student responses are no longer available to teachers and parents for review, while in many states even the aggregated scores aren't available soon enough to be useful anyway!).

EVALUATING EDUCATIONAL TESTING: FLAWED BY DESIGN

We all know that there's nothing new under the sun, and this is particularly true when it comes to what has been written against the overuse and misuse of scholastic testing. In fact, within a decade of the introduction of standardized testing for scholastic use, educators and education scholars were sending out warning signals about their overuse. In 1926, for instance, the National Society for the Study of Education published the following, strikingly modern-sounding critique:

> This Committee condemns emphatically the evaluation of the product of educational effort solely by means of subject-matter type examinations now prevalent in state and local school systems. We have reference specifically to the rigid control over the school curriculum exercised by those administrative examinations, which over-emphasized the memory of facts and principles and tend to neglect the more dynamic outcomes of instruction.[4]

Since that time, a veritable avalanche of research has built up that should have by now buried the issue beneath the weight of the evidence. In fact, many lengthy books have been written over the years dedicated entirely to showing that standardized tests are an inadequate measure of student learning and are crude instruments that have wrought incalculable damage to students, teachers, and schools, and to public education more broadly.[5]

And yet, as students, parents, and educators know all too well, the use of standardized testing in schools has only grown over the past several decades, to the point that even former proponents have shifted their position on the topic. One notable former proponent, the Texas commissioner of education, Republican Robert Scott, proclaimed in a 2012 meeting with members of the Texas State Board of Education that educational accountability based on high-stakes testing led to a "perversion" of the goal of public education.[6] Scott is right that testing is a perversion of sound educational practice, for it is precisely the children from the least advantaged families who need meaningful feedback from their teachers to gain the confidence that hard work pays off. The tests undermine both teachers' ability to provide such feedback and students' confidence in themselves as learners. In many schools, especially those serving poor students, the often losing battle to raise test scores produces humiliation and rage, as hard work doesn't seem to impact the one thing that counts in our current system: test results. Educators in schools serving poor students face threats of closure for failing to continually raise test scores, and so they too often find themselves making decisions against their professional judgment to, for example, drill students on test-taking skills, instead of engaging them in more meaningful subjects that might expand their worldly knowledge.[7] Society pays a price later, I suspect, in myriad ways, beginning with how the less advantaged may come to distinguish themselves from the "well-educated," developing a sense of social alienation and resentment.

Despite the evidence, however, testing has truly never gone out of style. In 2016, the Council of Great Schools reported that, during their thirteen years of schooling, students in urban school districts took approximately 112 tests, or eight per year.[8] The use of standardized tests for high-stakes purposes began to ramp up after the 1983 release of the federally commissioned report *A Nation at Risk*, which was followed by the bipartisan Goals 2000 act of 1994. Focused less on the achievement gap, the report condemned American education for its mediocre offerings and outcomes (mostly the drop in SAT averages and in international test averages between us and our international competitors). But the increase in the quantity and stakes of standardized tests exploded with the 2001 passage of No Child Left Behind legislation and further intensified with initiatives launched during the Obama era: Race to the Top and Common Core aligned tests. In addition to the state tests, schools and districts have begun to give several practice tests in the hopes of improving children's test-taking skills. Despite lip service from politicians and policymakers about the importance of providing students with a well-rounded, twenty-first-century education, it is not an exaggeration to say that raising student test scores in math and reading has become the primary focus in most schools—and that closing the test-based achievement gap has become education's proverbial white whale.

I dedicated a chapter to the topic of testing in my 2002 book, *In Schools We Trust*. I wish that I could say that the content is now outdated, but, unfortunately, as with the 1926 National Society for the Study of Education statement, the points I made then are only more pertinent today. In that chapter, I wrote about two related underlying problems embedded in how standardized tests are constructed that I think are important to recap here. First, there is the problem of *norming*.

THE RIGGED GAME OF RANKING

The period during which my PS 144 colleagues and I began questioning the validity of the tests also marked a most tumultuous time and place in the history of American public education. Divisive New York teacher strikes were in full swing during the late 1960s, based on understandable claims by radical Black and Latino activists that the majority-white unionized teaching force had low expectations for and little understanding of their children. They argued for local control. The 1968 strike was in protest of the dismissal of several white teachers, mostly union activists, from schools in a local control experimental district.[9] The strike caused a serious divide between parents and teachers. Test scores were a central part of the story.

The Elementary and Secondary Education Act (ESEA) of 1965 required the use of norm-referenced exams (direct descendants of IQ tests) to evaluate the progress of students receiving Title I funds, so schools that received the funds had to test students in grades three through twelve in reading and math at least once annually. Similar to today, minority students' low scores on standardized tests were used by civil rights activists in the 1960s as objective evidence that schools were failing to provide their children with an adequate education.

The achievement gap in scores between white students and students of color became a focal point in the discourse around testing. Closing that gap, then as today, was a goal for many civil rights leaders and policymakers from both the Right and the Left. It fueled the demand that all kids should be able to read at grade level by third grade—as defined by a test score of "3.7" (or, on current criterion referenced tests, by a label of "proficient" or "advanced") by the seventh month of third grade. Newspaper editors, school boards, concerned citizens, parents, and politicians clamored for higher standards, improved test scores, and an end to "illiteracy." Why, they complained, are half the kids below grade level no matter how much money we pour into the schools? Why shouldn't every child be able to read "on grade level" by the third grade?

Few citizens, or even educators, then or now, seem to acknowledge that test scores are a description of rank order, which remains static. The tests are designed to ensure that this is the case. Whether modeled after norm-referenced IQ tests or standards-based tests that have been in use since the 1990s, this is how test makers achieve and maintain "reliability."[10] The following is roughly how scholastic tests are created: A pool of items are developed and tested on a representative sample of students of the grade for which the test is intended. Each item's level of difficulty is established. Scores are compiled and rank order established, with some tweaking here and there to ensure that the items differentiate properly and produce the right rank order—ideally a bell curve, which is presumed to be the natural distribution of human traits.

But aha! During this process, some items prove to be bad items. Why? Because the wrong kids choose the right answers and the right kids choose the wrong ones. Psychometrically good items properly differentiate test takers. Items that everyone would get right, for instance, aren't useful because they don't differentiate even if they constitute what professionals believe to be evidence of appropriate third-grade skills. But the astounding discovery I made was that, like IQ tests, achievement-test makers know ahead of time *who* should get more right answers. If a great many schools prepare children for better than expected scores, items will be replaced and success will be redefined. As Nel Noddings's quote at the beginning of this chapter suggests, we will be back where we started with respect to the score distribution.

What makes an item easier or harder may involve adding more difficult passages, or devising trickier and more complex ways of wording the questions, or devising some other fix, not to better test students' aptitude or achievement but to get the distribution "right." Just altering a question ever so slightly can do the trick— creating items intended to distract a majority of test takers from choosing the "right" answer—will serve the purpose. The percentage of right or wrong answers varies enormously depending on how the test maker decides to present an item. Many of us may be able to correctly deduce, for example, who the sixteenth president of the United States is or isn't depending on what alternatives are offered in a multiple-choice question. By changing the wording slightly, test makers can make test takers appear to be either knowledgeable or ignorant—and the desired distribution is kept intact. It's not difficult to do. If I wanted a test that measured my three children in rank order, I could easily design an exam to favor or disadvantage each of the three. I don't believe that most test makers are racist or that they purposely rig the test with the intent of favoring white test takers over their nonwhite peers. And, yet, creating a test that produces what we have come to understand are "predictable" results is precisely what test makers *must* do as part of the norming process that ensures "stable" and "consistent" results, otherwise known as *reliability*.

When scores for too many low-income minority students rise on criterion-referenced tests, test makers suspect cheating; if it happens nationwide, it signals a need to renorm. On the norm-referenced tests, scores are proxies for percentage points, with an individual's ranking indicating how many test takers did better or worse. Therefore, no matter how much students collectively improve, half always score above and half below "grade level," when "grade level" is the 50th percentile.

Demanding that more kids get higher scores on standardized tests—be they IQ tests or achievement tests—is, under these circumstances, something like demanding that students line up faster so that more will be in the front half of the line. Tests have a built-in paradox: even as they are seen as more objective—and therefore more legitimate than teachers' judgment—they are also understood to be malleable enough to be renormed whenever it is deemed necessary.

There are many test proponents who understand and take advantage of this malleability to suit their political needs. For a time in the 1960s and 1970s, for example, when New York City used the same test year after year, scores inevitably went up each year. Therefore, savvy new superintendents began to order that new tests be developed and administered, knowing that would lower scores during the first part of their term in office and, thus, allowing them to take credit when scores miraculously rose again, as they inevitably do after two or three years in circulation.[11] Meanwhile, on the ground, tests have always had an outsize impact on the lives of students and educators, for when the scores drop back down, it is some hapless superintendent or principal who is fired, a group of teachers who is publicly humiliated by having his or her students' test scores publicized, and students who are prevented from earning a high school diploma.

Decades of being held to the fire for these unattainable goals should have by now diminished educators'—if not the public's—trust in such flawed instruments. And there is growing agreement, with a national test opt-out movement by families, that test scores are not statements of competence, no matter how we try to label them so. By definition, scores on standardized tests can never inform the public whether better learning and better teaching are taking place, whether children in America are fabulous readers or lousy ones. Alas, scholastic testing, whether normed or benchmarked, will never tell us anything but what test makers design them to tell us.

EMBEDDED BIAS

Since the 1990s, standardized tests have increasingly been used for high-stakes accountability purposes. No Child Left Behind legislation increased the stakes for schools and focused accountability on closing the persistent gap in test scores between wealthy and poor students, as well as between white students and students of color. Nearly two decades after the passage of NCLB, however, the National Assessment of Educational Progress data reveals that the gap has remained consistent along predictable demographic lines.[12] The truth is, as long as we continue to rely on traditional standardized tests, we will never close the gap between the haves and have-nots. The "gap" is built into the way items are designed, selected, or rejected based on whether or not they "fit" the statistical pattern that test makers are obligated to create in the name of *validity*.

Test validity refers to the extent to which a test measures what it's supposed to and requires a fairly clear preconceived idea about who the "good" students are—those likely, all else being equal, to do well by other criteria, including success on other tests taken now or in the future, and in their lives generally. Most tests use other tests as an external valuator.

It's worth reiterating here that current tests—even those labeled "new and improved" because they include more open-ended questions and use digital interfaces—have not fundamentally changed in this respect since the advent of IQ and scholastic testing a century ago. The developers of the original IQ tests, the mold for all other standardized tests, used their subjects' occupations as the external standard of validity. If doctors got more items wrong and plumbers got more right, the choice of items was not doing its job.[13] No surprise that, then as now, test takers from professional families do better on these tests than their working-class counterparts. With the SATs, research by the National Center for Fair &

Open Testing shows that for every $10,000 a family earns, their children's test scores go up incrementally.[14]

National admissions test expert, Jay Rosner, explains how this process works with college entrance exams, based on his access to the Educational Testing Service's (ETS) pool of possible test questions:

> Each individual SAT question ETS chooses is required to parallel the outcomes of the test overall. So, if high scoring test-takers—who are more likely to be white (and male, and wealthy)—tend to answer the question correctly in pretests, it's a worthy SAT item; if not, it's thrown out. Race and ethnicity are not considered explicitly, but racially disparate scores drive question selection, which in turn reproduces racially disparate test results in an internally reinforcing cycle.[15]

Any choice of subject matter, vocabulary, syntax, metaphors, word associations, and values presupposes a certain social and personal history. Personally, I'm probably good at guessing the right answers because I have been steeped in the subculture upon which the test makers build their system. I do not have to figure out what the test makers might want me to think, feel, or say; I am subliminally tuned in to the same world the tests are tapping, and as a result, I am predisposed to answer correctly. As in the case of a *New York Times* crossword maven, the right answers are lurking right beneath the surface—until one tries the crossword puzzle of a different elite. (Try doing British ones!) Similarly, when I was preparing for the National Teachers Exam in my mid-thirties, I recognized for the first time that my natural biases might not work for me on a test since my schooling history had not been mainstream. I had to engage in a more cautious and self-conscious process before filling in the boxes. At any age, being outside the culture a test is designed to tap imposes a handicap. At the very least, the need for such intellectual caution slows down "outlander" test takers.

When bias was first raised as a testing issue, test makers obligingly, but superficially, changed the content: some rural scenes were changed to urban ones, some complexions were darkened, a few archaic terms were eliminated; today, literary excerpts from far more nonwhite authors are included. But this is a hollow, irrelevant "victory" for test opponents. This is because, at bottom, test makers must create an instrument relying on a clear definition of what it means to be well educated, and such a definition presumes being a native of one particular, favored culture. Our backgrounds do discriminate between us to the advantage of some and the disadvantage of others—even on such mundane matters as making sense of a math problem or reading passage.

Let us consider a slightly altered example from a reading test I encountered some years ago:

> The children lived in a pleasant tree-lined street. One morning, trucks came and chopped down the trees in order to widen the road for a new four-lane highway. When spring came, the birds and squirrels, who used to live in the trees, did not come back.
>
> The question: When the truck came, the children were (a) excited, (b) bored, (c) sad, (d) tired.

How did I immediately know that the right answer was (c) "sad"? In real life, of course, children—rich or poor, Black or white—are unlikely to feel sad at the arrival of a truck. Depending on the circumstances they might be bored. Yet somehow I knew we were supposed to feel sad that the trees were going to be cut down, and intuitively picked the right answer without carefully examining the text or the logic of the alternatives. And I was right. Careful reading was just as likely to lead young children to the wrong answer. Yes, non-readers who randomly chose any of the four had a 25 percent chance of being right. But otherwise the question mainly differentiated children of one background from those of another. Though most of the middle-class white children agreed with my answer, the others were almost all sure that "excited" was correct. This kind of cultural discrepancy between the intuition of students from different backgrounds is generally something that passes unnoticed—and in fact makes the question about the trees a psychometrically sound item. Only when a pattern appears that interferes with our expectations—that is, the kids I expected to do well don't—is a red flag raised.

Thus, bias is in the nature of the testing tool. Any standardized tool in which neither the test taker nor their parent or their teacher is allowed to exercise human judgment—to explain, justify, adapt for this or that kid's particular background knowledge—carries such bias. It is necessarily steeped in prior cultural assumptions, norms that favor some kids over others. If all test takers responded the same way, the question would be a bad item, just as if the "wrong" people got it right, it would also be a bad item.

Ultimately, standardized testing engages students of color, and poor white children as well, in a cruel game that has been stacked against them. It dumbfounds them and their families by never allowing them to catch up. In the name of closing the test-score gap between white and minority students, both district public and charter schools serving predominantly poor students have become test-prep factories that attempt to "catch them up" at the price of missing science, music, drama, history, foreign languages, project time, clubs, or self-initiated activities.

Pretending that students of color and students in poverty should join a race to displace enough of their white counterparts in the proficient-to-advanced range of the normal curve—given no other major societal changes—is nothing short of cruel and unusual punishment. Those who argue that standardized testing helps create a more "meritocratic" society are not taking such a thought experiment far enough. Imagine what would happen if students in the Bronxville area of New York (very wealthy, predominantly white) started getting lower scores than their counterparts in the South Bronx (very poor Black and Brown students with a high percentage of English-language learners)? The test designers would be quick to "renorm" the test to "correct" such a clear "reliability threat."

Another trend—especially in many of the most popular charter school chains that have been praised for getting students from typically low-scoring groups to ace the tests—is teaching students that they must conform to dominant cultural norms in order to succeed. Students are made to believe that all they need is to have more "grit" in order to compete on equal footing with their wealthier peers. The implication here is that it is a moral weakness, a lack of discipline and will within themselves and their communities—their families and friends—that is the cause of their "failure." The "cure," according to these schools designed especially for poor students of color, is to train them to adopt the most superficial behaviors associated with middle-class norms, while robbing students of the real advantages of a well-rounded middle-class education.

Though these segregated and grossly unequal no-excuses schools (no family of means would send their children to these schools) give the illusion of helping poor minority students get ahead by raising their test scores, in reality, their stripped-down academic offerings and harsh, zero-tolerance disciplinary systems actually put poor kids at an even greater disadvantage. Such programs may prepare students to ace a particular test by drilling them on the basic content, but such intellectually devoid schooling does nothing to help the young build habits of mind and heart that will allow them to approach new situations, whether a new kind of scholastic exam or an unfamiliar life test. Even more problematic, these schools teach that the only path to success requires poor minority students to disavow themselves of their own cultural knowledge—shared customs and practices that have proven useful to them in life outside of school—in order to adopt instead the values and norms of mainstream (i.e., middle-class white) culture. This is not to say that there is nothing to learn from the dominant culture. After all, we argue throughout this book that all schools should resemble those that the most privileged seek out for their own children. But to deny poor children a well-rounded, middle-class education, while expecting them to embrace a culture that has throughout history barred their families and their ancestors—through violence, institutional systems, and laws—from joining their ranks, is tantamount to teaching them to disown their own cultural identities, their own sources of power.

If we are serious about empowering schools to play a meaningful role in leveling the playing field, we must accept that tests do nothing to address real wealth and opportunity gaps: gaps in access to enriching vacations to the sea shore or abroad; gaps in resources that wealthy families bring to their children's schools and whose financial contributions are enough to hire extra staff members, among other enhancements; gaps in access to basics such as adequate health care and healthy food, and on and on.

Imagine if instead of shaming poor children, along with their families, teachers, and schools, for not scoring well on standardized tests, we put the will and resources required toward addressing the real shame of being the country with the highest rates of infant mortality, child poverty, juvenile detention, and childhood housing and food insecurity in the industrialized world? Imagine if instead of wasting vast amounts of time, as well as human and monetary resources, on testing and test prep materials, instead of firing principals and teachers and closing schools, we invested in wrap-around services in schools: mental and physical health care for kids and their families, and other essentials that wealthy families take for granted. In short, if we are serious about closing the so-called achievement gap, we should work first to close our gaping social and economic equity gap.

COMMON CORE TESTS: NEW BUT NOT IMPROVED

The latest, computer-based tests, developed to align with Common Core standards, are intended to counter some of the problems critics have identified with the old paper-and-pencil exams.[16] Former secretary of education Arne Duncan promised, "For the first time, many teachers will have the state assessments they have longed for—tests of critical thinking skills and complex student learning that are not just fill-in-the-bubble tests of basic skills." Echoing Duncan's sentiments, designers of the Partnership for Assessment of Readiness for College and Careers (PARCC) and Smarter Balanced (SB) tests, the two most recent Common Core–aligned tests, boast that the improved tests replace the old multiple-choice questions with more sophisticated, computerized interfaces that allow students to respond to open-ended questions and show their aptitude for critical thinking. The PARCC and Smarter Balanced consortiums have contracted the same handful of companies responsible for bringing us the "inferior," pre–Common Core tests, including Pearson and McGraw Hill, who, according to a report by CNBC, have won $63 million and $72.5 million in contracts, respectively, as of the 2015–2016 school year.[17]

Though adding better questions to scholastic tests would certainly be a welcome development, upon review of both the PARCC and SB practice tests, it is clear that, aside from the computerized interface, not much has changed. First, one is struck by the fact that there seem to be just as many multiple-choice questions as ever. For example, a mostly positive assessment of the tests by the conservative Fordham Institute labeled 32 percent of questions on the Smarter Balanced math test and 43 percent on the reading test as "traditional multiple choice." However, that percentage rises to over 70 percent in each discipline on both the PARCC and the Smarter Balanced tests when factoring in what the report calls "multi-select" and "combination choice" questions, ones that "require a two-part answer—the first part being a multiple-choice question and a second part that asks students to provide evidence to support their first answer, which could take the shape of another multiple-choice question or a short, written response."[18]

Other problems with the computerized platform have been pointed out by experts in the field, such as Steven Rasmussen, a publisher of mathematics curricula and software. Rasmussen is hardly an anti-test crusader. By his own account, he was excited about the promises made by the PARCC and SB consortiums to introduce "technology-enhanced tests populated by high cognitive-demand tasks with interfaces that made smart use of digital tools."[19] He therefore approached the Smarter Balanced practice tests with optimism, hoping that "a $330 million investment of tax dollars from the U.S. Education Department and the pooled resources of state governments would produce a new generation of standardized tests for assessing student performance on the Common Core State Standards for Mathematics and English language arts—tests that would be better than traditional paper-and-pencil multiple-choice tests."[20] After taking the entire tenth-grade practice test offered by Smarter Balanced online, Rasmussen reported the following:

> What I found shocked me. This analysis of mathematics test questions posted online by Smarter Balanced reveals that, question after question, the tests violate the standards they are supposed to assess; cannot be adequately answered by students with technology they are required to use; are to be graded in such a way that incorrect answers are identified as correct and correct answers as incorrect. If the technology-enhanced items on the Smarter Balanced practice and training tests are indicative of the quality of the actual test . . . and Smarter Balanced tells us they are—the shoddy craft of the tests will directly and significantly contribute to students' poor scores.[21]

Assuming the test makers remedy these problems with new tests, they will still be constructed to create the ranking order problems previously described, assuring the same zero-sum outcome of test-score winners and losers.

In some ways, the new standards-based tests are worse than their norm-referenced predecessors. Since tests are now scored against a set benchmark and not a bell curve, test makers can place the cut-off at any level they choose. Perhaps this is why more and more students are failing these new tests (which couldn't happen with previous tests). On these tests, the proficiency "cut-offs" are based on test makers' judgment at best or a political decision at worst. This is why many middle-class white children have begun to fail as well. This trend has bolstered the common claim that public schools are failing everyone, not just poor and minority children. It has fueled, at least in part, the argument for more private, competitive education options for all.

As it is, these flawed instruments, regardless of format, play an essential part in perpetuating social and racial inequality, as they are still being used to make the most important decisions about students' futures: who gets held over, who can apply to the best schools, and who can graduate. When schools are threatened with sanctions or closure for not showing yearly test-score gains, it is low-scoring students—most likely to be African American and Latino children—who are more likely to be suspended, expelled, or pushed out of school regardless of their performance on the test. And requiring students to pass a test in order to receive their high school diploma has led too many students to drop out. The cost to these individuals, as well as the loss to society in human capital, is unacceptable. Research has shown, for example, that one in ten male high school dropouts ends up in prison—and that statistic becomes one in four for African American male dropouts—as opposed to one in thirty-five young men who have their diploma.[22]

Tests scores are also increasingly being used to decide whether teachers should get pay raises or keep their jobs, and whether schools should receive more resources or be closed. It justifies the loss of most Black teachers and many Black neighborhood schools.[23] Perhaps the most succinct way to summarize the dilemma we now find ourselves in regarding the ubiquity of educational testing is to quote Campbell's Law, which states: "Once a measure becomes the target, it ceases to be a good measure."[24]

AUTHENTIC ACCOUNTABILITY

Returning to the research I conducted with my PS 144 colleagues, I realize there was also an important collegial component to our work that put us in a better position to teach all our students well. In addition to providing reliable documentation of students' reading progress, the time we set aside to discuss various assessments helped foster a culture of shared knowledge and collaboration.

We got into the practice of conversing with and listening to our students and to one another. In fact, the most meaningful forms of assessment begin with listening, something that is entirely absent from standardized testing. I have learned this to be the case in my fifty-plus years working with children, their families, and my colleagues in traditional and progressive public schools. My classroom experiences have taught me that there are multiple ways of making sense of the world. Once I learned to listen, to control my urge to jump in and correct, I heard young children build arguments, putting together their observations and knowledge in logical and reasonable ways, arriving at conclusions that at first seemed absurd but that upon close listening often followed a scientist's line of reasoning.

Finding ways to help young people articulate their understanding, instead of immediately jumping in to "correct" their "mistakes" with my more informed, adult logic (or simply because I possessed the adult power to do so) was fascinating, as well as more educationally sound. Doing so opened up to me alternate ways of seeing and being in the world, even as it was at times frustrating. Suddenly, even seemingly objective subjects, such as math and science, offered exciting observations that sometimes conflicted with my intuition. Applying these insights to assessment of learning, upon listening to children explain their work, very often led me to understand that, more often than not, students who at first seemed to lack conceptual understanding were shown to be making fairly easily addressed technical mistakes, such as confusing the plus and minus symbol or not distinguishing between the letters *b* and *d*.

Such experiences led me to realize that the great virtue of democratic life is that we learn to exercise judgment and not seek what authorities claim is the one and only right answer. The opportunity to be in the presence of diverse views, mingling with people, including adults, whose experiences and viewpoints differ from our own is at the heart of democratic intellectual work. Until we share those different ways of thinking with each other, we can never claim to be anything close to "objective." Or rarely. Objectivity still mattered but was more complex than I originally thought, and democratic practices offer us a chance to lean into and practice this complexity.

When, in 1974, my colleagues and I started Central Park East (CPE) elementary school as an experiment in public education for democracy, we were influenced by the open-classroom movement that emphasized developing individual interests in authentic social settings, more specifically, by Lillian Weber's Open Corridor model, which emphasized teacher collaboration. We were all also deeply influenced by Dewey's writing on education and democracy, in which he argued that we learn through experience and in the company of others, especially those with whom we differ, and that these are the principles underlying democracy. As he writes in *Democracy and Education*, "Democracy is . . . primarily a mode of *associated living* [my emphasis] of conjoint communicated experience."[25] The closest most schools come to teaching democratic values is to have students read canned textbook passages on topics related to American civics, but Dewey insisted that democracy grows from social interaction—shared experiences, dialogue, and grappling with disagreement among individuals from different backgrounds.

My colleagues and I chose to govern CPE and every school I started after that collaboratively, not only because we thought it was the best way to model for students what democratic practices looked like but also because we have always held fast to the conviction (perhaps against all odds) that democracy is the most effective form of governance. In starting CPE 1, staff puzzled out how to develop the curriculum and assessments that would allow for the most flexibility within each classroom, while also creating a culture of common values that would be conducive to *associative living* throughout the school. We understood from the beginning that standardized testing ran directly counter to the kind of teaching and learning that supports the cultivation of empowered citizenship. But in 1974, with the support of a strong district superintendent, it was still possible to dodge the tests and develop our own assessments that were grounded in the actual curriculum and drew on teachers' knowledge of individual students.

Years later, at Central Park East Secondary School (CPESS), staff developed the Five Habits of Mind and the Graduation by Portfolio performance assessments. For families nervous about how their children might fair in an alternative high school setting, we did some simple prepping and explained in writing and in face-to-face sessions our objections to standardized tests; we explained the degree of official measurement error that occurs with tests and showed families a simpler, more accurate way to assess student learning. The goal of arriving at a shared understanding by the student, the family, and the school regarding the student's competence was critical. Where perspectives differed, it was worth exploring—together. Getting at "the truth" was a collaborative task, not a fiat from above. Even when there was one clear, definitive answer, as there generally is in math, for instance, it was nevertheless foolish, even inefficient to brush aside alternative explanations and accounts. It was with all this in mind that Mission Hill School adopted some of the assessment systems used at both CPE and at CPESS, built around our daily classroom practices in which students were expected to challenge their own thinking, as well as that of others—books, friends, and teachers alike.

At bottom, there are two points about accountability I started I hope to have conveyed in this chapter. The first is about accountability for student learning. Learning, like democracy itself, is a social endeavor. Even when students work independently, they are drawing on their associative experiences and funds of shared cultural knowledge, building on existing academic and social understanding. Meaningful assessments, therefore, also generally include a social component. They require close observation and deep listening, the ability to weigh evidence against multiple measures with input from others who know the individual well.

The second point is about the nature of *authentic* accountability—that is, accountability for meeting the actual educational and professional aims set by those working day in and day out with individual students and their families. In all the schools I have worked and had a hand in starting, authentic accountability came from creating a culture of integrity at the ground level. Schools that create collegial professional communities tend to foster a culture in which everyone feels accountable to one another and responsible for the success of the school community as a whole. For all the reasons discussed in this chapter (as well as myriad other related problems that readers can easily learn about by accessing the large body of scholarship on the topic), high-stakes testing runs directly counter to the kind of intellectual work that schools for democracy strive to provide for students and undermines the trust and kinds of relationships necessary for cultivating democratic values.

MOVING BEYOND TESTS

AUTHENTIC ACCOUNTABILITY IN PRACTICE

Emily Gasoi

> I am profoundly suspect of prevailing claims of education progress measured only by test scores, but I am equally hungry for a deep accountability framework that speaks ethically and honestly about the challenges and accomplishments of schools.
>
> —MICHELLE FINE
> in *Educating for the 21st Century*[1]

LEARNING, LIKE DEMOCRACY ITSELF, *is a social endeavor.* Keeping this principle in mind, Mission Hill School staff designed almost all our assessments of student learning to include a social component. In kindergarten through fifth grade, students kept individual portfolios that they shared with their families at our biannual family conferences. Students were responsible for creating labels for their portfolio work with the understanding that what they wrote would have to say something about their work to an outside audience. In our case, the audience was primarily their teachers and family members, but as students grew older, depending on their future school and work trajectories, keeping a well-organized portfolio would be an important applicable skill.

For reading assessments, the school used a set of leveled books, organized by degree of difficulty, from simple, phonetically focused texts for emergent readers to more complex texts for advanced readers. We kept track of student reading fluency and comprehension based on triannual one-on-one reading interviews, and we recorded students' reading (at that time, on a cassette player!), so in addition to an ongoing written evaluation, teachers, children, and families had an audio record of students' progress as readers which students and families could take home at the end of their time at Mission Hill School. For math we had each student complete the Boston Public School Benchmark, and for a time, we also used the Vermont Exemplars, a set of open-ended math tasks that requires students to show their problem-solving strategies and, thus, their conceptual understanding of each item. The exemplars include rubrics and samples of what student work looks like at each level of the rubric to guide teachers' assessment of their students' work. After that, we conducted a similar one-on-one interview in which the student explained his or her way of thinking about and solving the problems.

Three times a year, at the end of every schoolwide theme, students present their work through performances and curated displays. When my second and third graders decided to recreate the tomb of the Mayan monarch, King Pacal, in our class coatroom, students had to share what they learned in order to explain the exhibit, tailoring their explanation to the particular audience, depending on whether it was younger or older students from other classrooms, adult visitors to the school, or their families as part of our culminating performance "assessment."

Reviewing the video footage from this culminating project, I see that students made a pamphlet explaining the facts and history of King Pacal's tomb. Samantha and Keith handed them out and directed families to the tomb entrance, where students took turns leading the tour, flashlights in hand. Inside the tomb, students explained the contents, why certain items were buried with kings and

not with common folk, and then they took questions. Their excitement was discernable, even as they maintained a "professional" (for seven- and eight-year-olds!) docent demeanor, something they learned from our many class outings to Boston's Museum of Fine Arts. After the tour, students sat as if on a panel at an academic conference and fielded questions from their parents about both the content of their study and the process of creating a mock tomb. The night culminated with students reading aloud from their project journals to give families an idea of connections they made—personal and literary—as well as facts they learned about ancient Mayan culture.

As mentioned in previous chapters, middle school students at Mission Hill School have three years to compile more structured portfolios in six disciplines: literature, mathematics, humanities, art, science, and "beyond the classroom," which focused on an interest the student pursued outside of school.[2] At various points throughout their seventh- and eighth-grade years, students present their work in each of these portfolio subjects (usually two at a time) to a committee (composed of the student's advisor, the subject teacher(s), a sixth-grade helper, a community member, and family members) that uses a rubric based on the Five Habits of Mind to guide a collective assessment of the students' presentation and work.

Following the presentation, the student responds to any questions the committee members may have before leaving the room. The committee members then discuss their observations, lingering questions, doubts, and so forth, all while consulting the subject rubric and listening to any additional information about the student's work the subject teacher might find it pertinent to add. Once the committee has come to consensus on whether or not the student passed with or without revisions, the student is called back into the room and the committee explains the reasoning behind its assessment. Students have an opportunity to revise work if they did not pass the first time, but eighth graders must receive a passing evaluation in all six (now five) portfolios in order to graduate.[3]

The portfolio process is intense and instructive for all involved. Over the course of two years, everyone, including family and community members, cannot help but become deeply invested in the student's progress. Every time a student sends out work for review to committee members and then presents that work, the adults on the committee become more familiar with the student's way of working and making decisions, and his or her growing ability to articulate more nuanced and an evolving understanding ideas in the focus domain. Instead of receiving a single score intended to sum up some arbitrarily benchmarked level of achievement, students who do not pass all criteria in a given subject are required to revise some or all of their work, which then is reevaluated by the committee, only deepening everyone's learning. The high level of formative value to the adults involved, and the self-efficacy and real knowledge gained by students throughout the portfolio process, stands in great contrast with the standardized tests that some students—by the time they reach eighth grade—have taken for five consecutive years.

In 2008, I conducted interviews with fifteen MHS alumni to find out what, if anything, they remembered about the process, specifically, if they felt it had influenced their decisions and ability to navigate as they went on through higher levels of education and work. All the participants remembered their experience (mostly the emotional impact, e.g., feeling nervous, worried, overwhelmed, disappointed, or proud), and many of them were able to articulate how it had influenced them after leaving the school. Alumni raised a range of specific examples: several mentioned that presenting six portfolios before a committee of adults had made them confident public speakers; others spoke about how high school felt easy afterward because nothing compared to the intensity of the portfolio process; still others mentioned that they learned how to manage their time and organize their work. What was striking, however, was the unanimity with which this sample of alumni spoke about the state tests and college entrance exams they had taken, essentially describing them as hurdles to be cleared and left behind. As one graduate explained:

> I feel like I don't get something in return [from tests] besides my scores. With portfolio presentations, you really learn how to be a good presenter, how to . . . put your work together and present for your teachers—I was really proud of myself, I remember [after presenting], even though I had to redo some stuff.

Something that all of these MHS assessment practices have in common is that they require students to explain their thinking and, in the case of middle school portfolios, defend their work. All of them require interaction between students and their assessors, allowing students to articulate their theories, their struggles, and their breakthroughs in the course of demonstrating understanding, which in turn provides the assessor(s) with a more nuanced picture of students' learning. In addition, unlike standardized testing, these assessments help students build strong work habits and skills that will serve them as they move through higher levels of education, the world of work, and beyond. Skills such as working collaboratively, public speaking and presentation, being able to defend one's ideas, considering how others might perceive your work, and critical and creative thinking are all considered twenty-first-century skills, but they are also timeless skills that we knew would serve students well as they left us to begin the next chapter in their lives, whatever that might be and wherever that might take them.

THE NATURE OF AUTHENTIC ACCOUNTABILITY

During my last two years working at Mission Hill School, I became coordinator for the middle school portfolio process. I had the opportunity during those years to get a close-up view of the process and gather input from all parties: the students, their teachers, student advisors, and committee members. Admittedly, the process was at times logistically cumbersome, even onerous for some students and their committees when a student had to revise and re-present multiple portfolios. But in the end, it was one of the most satisfying aspects of my work at the school. I can say without qualification, for all the reasons outlined in the previous section, that the portfolio process is an overwhelmingly positive and enduring educative experience for all.

In fact, I was so impressed with the system of graduation by portfolio that when I went off to graduate school in 2005 and had to come up with a dissertation topic, I originally planned to do a longitudinal study of the impact of the portfolio process on Mission Hill School alumni as they went on to higher levels of education and beyond. My dissertation research eventually evolved into the study of school-based assessment and accountability more broadly. I was, therefore, especially interested in following how things unfolded in my home "state"—the District of Columbia—when the restrictive accountability regulations under No Child Left Behind were loosened under the 2015 Every Student Succeeds Act (ESSA), giving states more control to design slightly less rigid accountability plans.

Under ESSA, states are responsible for developing a plan to meet the law's accountability requirements by fall 2017.[4] The law still requires states to mandate standardized testing in grades three through eight and in grade ten but allows them to reduce the weight that student test scores hold in the assessment of overall school quality. There is also a section of the act that allows up to seven states to include as part of their plan an alternative accountability system through the Innovative Assessment Demonstration Authority pilot program. I was hopeful that the District of Columbia's Office of the State Superintendent of Education (OSSE), which was responsible for drafting the new state accountability plan, would take advantage of all the opportunities ESSA offers to expand the conception of what it means to be an "effective and high quality" school. Unfortunately, my hopes (and those of many other district educators, families, and school advocates) were soon dashed.

OSSE posted its proposed plan online in late January 2017 and held a series of open forums throughout February, inviting stakeholders to ask questions and voice concerns. Before attending the first forum, I reviewed the plan and was shocked to find that it proposed to count student scores as 80 percent of a school's overall evaluation, with 40 percent of that attributed to student growth and another 40 percent attributed to "achievement" (i.e., scoring "proficient" or better) on standardized tests. The other 20 percent was split between attendance, student retention rates, and academic gains for English-language learners (ELL).[5]

What was particularly surprising about this decision was that ESSA allows states to reduce the weight of testing to 55 percent, leaving room for schools to innovate and meet another of the act's requirements, which is to offer students a well-rounded education. Despite the alternate accountability opportunities ESSA opened up, I was deeply concerned to find that the OSSE plan did not consider any programming that might contribute to a well-rounded education—including arts, STEM, maker spaces, Expeditionary Learning, clubs, and student-initiated or project based learning—in its evaluation of school quality.

I attended two of the public forums and another open session for public testimonials that took place the week before the school board voted on the plan. All three sessions had impressive attendance, both in terms of numbers and diversity. At the first meeting, held in February 2017, a high school ELL teacher expressed utter frustration over not being able to address the actual needs of her students. Many of them, she explained, have made real, documented progress in their language acquisition but still could not score "proficient" on the PARCC exam. Though the PARCC is designed to be an improvement on the last generation of standardized tests, they are, nevertheless, still developed using the same culturally biased methods Deb discusses in the previous chapter.

Further, even the math exam is text heavy, making it especially challenging for ELL students. Nevertheless, this teacher's school, which serves 85 percent ELL students, has depended on these test scores to receive a good evaluation according to the old, and now the new, state accountability plan.

A parent spoke out, asking, "Where's the willingness to be bold? I see nothing here except the same old tests, when so many of our kids have very real, pressing needs. Why not hold schools accountable for wraparound services so kids *and* their families can be well fed and healthy?" An education advocate spoke up about the harm that testing has done by gutting the curriculum serving poor, minority students, and on and on and on it went, an hour past the time when the meeting was supposed to end. During the two public forums I attended, not one parent, teacher, or concerned citizen spoke positively of the plan. And in more than three hours of testimonials from approximately sixty speakers at the public hearing, only one was an advocate of the plan. Despite this, the District State Board of Education passed the plan with only minor changes, including a 10 percent reduction in the weight of the tests in evaluating schools, which is now at 70 percent instead of 80.[6]

At the last public forum, which took place about a month after the first one, I asked the state superintendent why, given the overwhelming public opposition to the plan expressed by a range of stakeholders, OSSE wouldn't consider taking advantage of ESSA's flexibility to use multiple measures of school quality. She explained that the district would not be able to devise a system of data collection and analysis for alternative forms of assessment before the plan was due. Nor was there a strategy or budget included in the plan for pursuing a more diversified accountability system in the future.

Perhaps this lack of interest in taking advantage of more broadly defined notions of accountability shouldn't have surprised me. After all, states have been subjected to nearly two decades of high-stakes testing, which is now a fairly entrenched frame of reference for judging student, teacher, and school success. Nevertheless, ESSA's loosening of the high-stakes strings attached to testing, coupled with the voices that I heard at the public forums that opposed the use of resources on test-based accountability and on using tests to make important decisions, gave me hope that a shift toward more meaningful and dynamic accountability measures may indeed be on the horizon.

But such a shift will only be as viable as are the alternative forms of assessment that replace the tests. What options might the district and other states consider? There are numerous models of holistic accountability systems—some well established, some new—that are worthy of emulation. In the following section, I profile three such models at the consortium, district, and state levels.[7]

THE NEW YORK PERFORMANCE STANDARDS CONSORTIUM

As Deb explains in chapter 5, authentic accountability means "meeting the actual educational and professional aims set by those working day in and day out with individual students and their families." That is, accountability measures must serve the needs of each school community and not the reverse. One well-established alternative system that supports bottom-up, integrated accountability practices was developed in 1998 as part of the New York Performance Standards Consortium. The NYPSC consists of thirty-eight small, alternative high schools, many of which are members of the Coalition of Essential Schools in the early 1990s.

Though each school in the consortium has its own unique features, all are rooted in the Coalition of Essential Schools' Ten Principles (see appendix). CES principles guide curriculum development (*depth over breadth*), pedagogy (*student as worker, teacher as coach*), assessment of student learning (*demonstration of mastery*), collegiality and shared leadership (*commitment to the entire school*), and school culture (modeling *democracy and equity*). This means that all NYPSC schools agree to craft curriculum that leads to active learning through project-based assignments, original research and experiment design, and multiple modes of approaching and completing assignments. The network-wide assessment system is designed to support NYPSC schools as they work to provide students with a high-quality education in alignment with CES principles and other school-based goals and values.

The New York State Board of Regents has granted NYPSC schools the right to replace all but one New York State Regents Exam with rigorous performance assessments. Specific performance assessments are determined by students and teachers in each school based on curriculum content and student interests, but the tasks in the four disciplines use common guidelines and rubrics to create reliability across sites. Students are required to competently complete in-depth research projects and papers that demonstrate their ability to think like historians, write literary essays that demonstrate analytic thinking, and show high levels of conceptual knowledge in math and science through application in real-world scenarios. Schools add on additional required tasks specific to their population and school mission. Drawing on the Central Park East Secondary School's graduation process, the NYPSC modeled its assessments after a PhD defense, in which students must defend their work and field questions from a panel of reviewers.

To monitor school quality across the network, the NYPSC has established a Performance Assessment Review Board to regularly evaluate the schools. The PARB, composed of educators, test experts, researchers, and members of the legal and business world, monitors the performance-based assessment system in party by systematically sampling student work. Its role is to help schools reflect on whether or not their practices align with their goals for their school and their students, and to support them to address areas of misalignment. The reviews are formative, supporting membership schools in their already ongoing process of self-reflective improvement.

LOS ANGELES UNIFIED SCHOOLS DISTRICT: SCHOOL QUALITY REVIEW

In 2007, the United Teachers of Los Angeles (UTLA) and the local Belmont community, in agreement with the Los Angeles school district (LAUSD), launched a small Pilot School network in what became known as the Belmont Zone of Choice. The BZC was modeled after the Boston Pilot School Network, and the Center for Collaborative Education, along with other local education-partnership organizations, was involved in helping their West Coast sister network get started.

In 2009, encouraged by the positive feedback from the school staff and families involved in the BZC experiment, the UTLA and LAUSD agreed to expand the number of pilot schools and over time created multiple pathways for any LAUSD public schools to opt in to several distinct autonomous networks.[8] At this time, Los Angeles is perhaps the only unified districts in the United States to provide all public schools the option of becoming an autonomous school, and as of the publication of this book, there are over ninety self-selecting, self-governed schools taking part in the initiative.

Pilot Schools are granted greater autonomy in exchange for increased accountability. Therefore, in addition to being held responsible for administering many of the district assessments and the state test, they are also expected to design their own in-house assessments to track student learning and growth. In addition to its school-based assessments, CCE developed an evaluation system for pilot schools called the School Quality Review (SQR), an in-depth and dynamic process that, when appropriately executed, engages all parties in an improvement-oriented cycle of reflection, dialogue, and planning.[9] Ideally, the SQR process involves all members of the school community in an annual internal review, reflecting on the extent to which their practices align with or support the school mission and the four elements of the SQR rubric: school-wide instructional focus, community engagement, implementation of autonomies, and capacity for growth.[10]

An interactive accountability system, the SQR process relies on strong communication among school staff during preparation for the review and between staff and external review team members once the review process is underway. After a school has compiled materials related to their efforts to meet the rubric criteria, an external review team, composed of representatives from the school's district zone, the teachers' and administrators' unions, and community-based organizations, studies the school's materials before conducting an intensive school visit. During the school visit, the review team might conduct interviews with representative members of the school community, observe in classrooms, and take note of the overall school climate. The review team then provides the school with a report that includes findings and recommendations. Once the school staff has reviewed the recommendations and provides feedback, the committee finalizes the report and shares it with the Pilot Schools Steering Committee (PSSC) responsible for deciding what renewal recommendation to give the school.[11]

THE NEW HAMPSHIRE PERFORMANCE ASSESSMENT FOR COMPETENCY EDUCATION (PACE)

In 2015, New Hampshire began piloting their Performance Assessment for Competency Education (PACE) in four districts that demonstrated the capacity and interest to lead the charge. The initiative has grown over the years, with more than thirty districts opting in as of the 2017–2018 school year. If all goes as planned, New Hampshire will eventually have the first statewide alternative accountability system in the country. As such, PACE has become a national model, inspiring architects of the 2015 Every Student

Succeeds Act to include in the law an Innovative Assessment Program encouraging up to seven states to follow New Hampshire's lead in developing innovative accountability plans.

As the name suggests, the PACE system prioritizes performance assessments that require students to demonstrate understanding of assessed content as well as competence in a range of other skills and dispositions, such as creativity, collaboration, and critical and flexible thinking. The system also emphasizes individual student competency—students' ability to show what they've learned—over traditional grading systems. This has led several participating schools and districts to begin the process of eliminating letter grades and even grade-level assignations for classes, grouping students instead by their levels according to locally developed and common state competency benchmarks.

One of the most dramatic improvements that the PACE system makes is to significantly reduce the frequency of student testing, only administering standardized tests once at the elementary, middle, and high school levels. In place of testing, students in grades three through eight engage in competency-based performance assessments that have been designed by local educators and that are grounded in work in which they have actually been engaged.

Underlying the strong momentum New Hampshire's new accountability initiative has gained among educators is the manner in which the initiative has been rolled out. Instead of rushing to implementation, PACE has been introduced in multiple, sensible phases. While the first districts piloted PACE in 2015, the state began to engage interested districts in professional development as early as 2012. This helped generate excitement and build expertise among practitioners prior to undertaking the first stages of the plan.

Further, adoption of the PACE system is not mandated. Rather, districts apply to be included in a growing consortium of districts that in turn act as both models and collegial support systems to each cohort of new joiners. Finally, the state has developed a system of differentiated and ongoing support based on district capacity at the time that they join the consortium. For example, when districts apply, they fill out a "Readiness Matrix" intended to determine their level of preparedness and specific areas where they might need support. Once districts become part of the consortium, state-level support systems are in place to build district expertise in how to design, administer, and reliably score high-quality performance assessments, aligned with state curriculum frameworks, among other benchmarks.

All three of the accountability systems presented in this section, whether assessing student learning or school quality, have taken the bold step of attempting to act on what education researchers and practitioners have known for decades about the inextricable relationship between teaching, learning, and assessment; about the importance of educator buy-in and direct input into meaningful accountability practices; about how humans learn and how to cultivate a culture of internal accountability within schools; and about what kinds of student learning and school practices are worth assessing.

This is not to say that these more dynamic systems are without flaws. For example, in conversations with a representative from the LAUSD Office of School Choice and a director of one of the local school-partnership organizations, I learned that the SQR process is often truncated and superficial in many of the newer pilot schools. Though the original pilots were small, community-based, and teacher-led schools that were invested in reflective practices associated with the SQR accountability system, the accelerated pace at which LAUSD then moved to scale up pilots and multiple other initiatives focused on school choice has led to predictable challenges.

District schools that have opted to join the pilot network since 2009 started out with varying levels of expertise, capacity, and

interest in becoming more reflective professional communities. Further, pilots have begun to lose one of the essential autonomies needed to cultivate a professional learning community: the ability to hire their own school leader and staff, who are likely to buy in to the school mission. This has not squared well with the job-security priorities of the teachers' union. Finally, the pilot initiative, lumped in as one among many school-choice initiatives in the country's second-largest school district, is severely under-staffed and underresourced, causing challenges regarding the logistics of assessing so many autonomous schools but also in terms of gaining buy-in to the intensive accountability process in which they agree—at least on paper—to engage.

And though New Hampshire seems to be avoiding all these mistakes in their slow, methodical, and focused roll-out of the PACE initiative, it is still too early to tell what might happen next. This is especially true given the fact that a new conservative school commissioner, whom one New Hampshire educator described in a personal communication with me as having an "anti-schools outlook," has taken over. As Deb will explain in the next chapter, one unsupportive school-system leader can put an end to other-wise strong school improvement initiatives.

It is also true that none of these in-depth accountability processes produces numeric data that can be efficiently gleaned in a single scan, and thus demand a greater input of time and energy on the part of all involved. But the value of the data they do produce both in terms of assessing and informing educator practices and student learning make the intensive investment worthwhile. In fact, it is precisely the investment that those most impacted put into these assessments that make the process of implementation and the results more enriching, more useful, and, ultimately, more valid than those garnered from standardized tests.

All three systems are based on assessments that are integrated into the fabric of school practices. This means that they offer students the opportunity to demonstrate knowledge and skills based on content they have actually studied and that is rooted in a school culture and values with which they have had an opportunity to become versed. Further, all of these assessments support inquiry, project-based learning, offering students a range of ways to show knowledge and skills, many of which are not captured by standardized tests. In short, these in-depth assessments tap higher-order thinking and problem solving, providing meaningful data while also strengthening student learning and teachers' professional capacities.

In sum, though standardized tests produce data that is more efficiently captured by an oversight agency such as OSSE, their continued overuse lowers the quality of education that students receive and misrepresents the hard work of students, teachers, and their schools. Test-based accountability encourages schools to emphasize outmoded instructional practices, such as prioritizing rote learning and correct answers over inquiry, holding all students to a one-size-fits-all benchmark, discouraging collaboration, undervaluing creative and critical thinking, and assessing discrete, decontextualized skills, all of which runs counter to what is now being touted as twenty-first-century teaching and learning.

BUILDING A CULTURE OF SCHOOL-BASED ACCOUNTABILITY

In my review of the District of Columbia's ESSA accountability plan, something stood out to me: in addition to an over-reliance on test-based indicators, there was a complete absence of indicators that draw on teacher knowledge of student learning or perceptions of school quality. We cannot continue to run a system that sidesteps the professionals with whom we are entrusting our children, our nation's future, as a vital source of information. Again, the qualitative and hybrid accountability systems outlined in the previous section may be unwieldy and require more time, but as the examples of school networks and districts participating in performance assessments show, engaging teachers in the process is entirely possible and makes it more likely that assessments align with school practices and actual student learning. I learned firsthand during my years at Mission Hill School how important it was for teachers to be actively and meaningfully engaged in assessing students' academic and affective growth, both in service of improving teachers' ability to meet individual student needs and to improve their sense of investment in their school and their profession.

But the lack of trust in teachers to make important decisions related to their own teaching and assessing practices has grown in tandem with the rise of high-stakes testing. There has been an incredible boom in scripted and computer-based curricula, mass-produced assessments, and even "character building" materials that essentially dictate much of what teachers can think, do, or prioritize in the classroom, regardless of what their own judgment might tell them. Not only have these trends led to the loss of teachers' invaluable on-the-ground expertise in reformers' efforts to improve schooling for all children, but such practices run directly counter to fostering a culture of accountability within schools.

One of the underacknowledged problems with defining school success in terms of test scores is that it discourages school leaders and staff from being accountable to their own organizational values and mission; it too often creates in schools a defensive, reactionary approach to accountability, distracting staff from attending to the actual needs of the school community. A teacher friend of mine, Zia Hassan, encountered this problem when he applied for elementary classroom positions in the Washington, DC, area. At the conclusion of each interview, he asked his interviewers one question that he felt revealed whether the school culture supported meaningful teaching and learning. The question was "What is a project that you've seen from students in the last month that amazed you?"

The responses he received from all but one or two schools were discouraging but reflective of the narrowly defined conception of education, which I also found reflected in the District of Columbia

ESSA plan. For example, one interviewer responded, "Hm. Interesting question. I think it's reading. Yeah, reading has been the project that has amazed me the most."

Another offered, "We track our students' reading levels on a big bulletin board outside. What's amazing has been watching their growth." And still another explained, "Well, we've moved away from fluffy projects. They do little to increase student achievement and understanding. We're more interested in cultivating students that can analyze and write about text."

Zia's poignant account speaks to the austerity that the current system of accountability has induced in a majority of public schools. Even in schools serving a predominantly privileged student body, many principals have come to view anything but "basics," such as reading and math, as a luxury. But the problem is more pronounced in schools serving students who score poorly on standardized tests, where educators, under intense pressure to raise scores, are not afforded time or space to think beyond students' literacy and math data. Given the wide range of intellectual and affective needs students bring with them to any classroom, regardless of demographics or zip code, as well as the complex demands they will encounter in college, the workplace, and as citizens in their communities and the world, it is insufficient to use such a reductive—indeed, an *impoverished*—conception of what constitutes quality education for accountability purposes.

Authentic accountability begins with the cultivation of a culture in which everyone feels responsible to one another and to the success of the school community as a whole. In a hierarchical organizational structure, supervisors hold workers accountable for completing various tasks to the supervisor's satisfaction. In a democratic organizational structure, on the other hand, each team member holds themselves and their colleagues accountable for meeting individually or collectively determined goals. *Authentic accountability*, then, is predicated on schools creating a culture of professional integrity among staff. In order to build such a culture, public school leaders need a high degree of autonomy to define and assess student, teacher, and school success.

Mission Hill School has developed a strong culture of internal accountability that relies on intensive collegial communication and trust. When defining norms at the school's founding, Deb envisioned a setting in which communication would support the cultivation of tight-knit relationships among members of the school community: teachers would know every child by name and feel a sense of responsibility, not only for the students in their classroom but for every individual in the school; all families should feel a strong connection with at least one staff member; and staff would share practices on a regular basis and feel part of a supportive professional community.

Toward this end, Deb stipulated that MHS should remain a small school and that the class size should never exceed twenty-two. To Deb, this also encouraged a culture of authentic accountability, as she explained to me in a 2011 interview:

> If the staff is making many of the decisions, then [the] success or failure of decisions has an effect on everybody. . . . Accountability for your classroom requires you to take responsibility, to make decisions about your class. But it also requires . . . that your class is not behind closed doors, that the work that is done in the class is shared with others, and you're open to feedback. You have to be able to explain your work to families and colleagues at family conferences, through kids presenting their work, etc. . . . and it depends on what the word "accountability" means. If you mean accounting for each child, then you have to write letters home . . . to families and to your colleagues to explain what you're doing and defend it just like kids defend their work with portfolios. You have to be willing and able to persuade people. So [accountability] is about the public-ness of the school.

As Deb explains, transparent, honest, and frequent communication among colleagues and between the school and its constituents is a defining component of MHS's internal accountability practices.

During a team meeting with colleagues I remember keeping notes on students—*Sheila has really taken on leadership for creating the artifacts for our mock tomb; Gabby has started to be able to read her own and others' ancient Egypt encyclopedias; Keith hasn't yet found his place in this study, he wanders around the room spending 5 minutes looking through a book on hieroglyphs, 10 minutes observing what others are doing*, etc. I knew my colleagues and I would take time at our weekly team meetings to share these kinds of informal assessments of individual students. We compared notes, looked for patterns and standouts, areas where we should step back and where we should take things deeper. We talked about individuals who were thriving and others who needed more support, and we shared our strategies for addressing the various problems that arose. What we came to understand in those meetings was that no one was more knowledgeable about the work we were doing with the kids in our care than we were, and so our time to confer and share with one another, to air our misgivings, challenges, and triumphs, was invaluable. Thousands of formal and informal collegial interactions throughout the school year are at the heart of smart practice that keeps teachers from burning out. Such intense collaboration evolves into a culture of shared responsibility for student learning, for upholding the school mission and values, and for knowledge-sharing that benefits the entire school community.

All the assessment processes described in this chapter are time consuming and require increased input and expertise from teachers and, in some cases, from the entire school community. This is considered a drawback by superintendents and others who are responsible for providing stakeholders with district- or state-level accountability data. But, I argue, the depth of involvement from practitioners, as well as from the wider community, is precisely what makes these demonstration- and discussion-based methods so powerful. Mandating overly broad and shallow assessments not only undermines deep teaching and learning; it also speaks volumes about what we value. If we value and hope to inculcate in future generations democratic practices and dispositions, then we need accountability measures that support those practices and dispositions.

Mission Hill School teachers certainly feel accountable for students' academic learning, but how absurd to think that it should be in the service of producing better data! Our concern regarding students' acquisition of academic knowledge is folded into a larger concern that they use such knowledge to formulate their own big ideas and become obsessed with their own burning questions. We want them to leave us feeling as if they have an important stake and a role to play in society, and we feel accountable for educating students so they are more likely to become well-rounded and conscientious individuals who see themselves as empowered citizens. As the opening paragraph of the MHS mission statement asserts:

> The task of public education is to help parents raise youngsters who will maintain and nurture the best habits of a democratic society [and] be smart, caring, strong, resilient, imaginative and thoughtful. It aims at producing youngsters who can live productive, socially useful and personally satisfying lives, while also respecting the rights of all others. The school, as we see it, will help strengthen our commitment to diversity, equity and mutual respect.[5]

After nearly two decades of data-driven reforms, too many of us have become trapped into thinking narrowly about what we hope for our students and, therefore, for our future. We can no longer afford to have such meager expectations. Yes, school should equip students with the academic and affective know-how and social networks that will help them to navigate college, if they should choose that route. This is especially important for those students who would be the first in their family to attend. But we need to allow ourselves to dream beyond the practical. Again, I argue, this is especially important for students whose life circumstances too often land them in schools where they are kept on the straight and narrow, smothered in what they're told are the "basics" and fed a pre-packaged "American Dream" to pursue, hindering them from dreaming their own dreams.

Given this, what reforms and conditions would support the proliferation of schools with the capacity and vision to cultivate a strong culture of authentic accountability?

CHAPTER 7

WHAT HAPPENS TO DEMOCRATIC EDUCATION DEFERRED?

THE RISE OF THE FREE ENTERPRISE SOCIETY

Deborah Meier

> Public education is predicated on the notion that you're con-
> cerned about other people's kids just as much as your own
> kids. . . . But all of this privatizing, profit obsession, all of this
> preoccupation with short-term gain has pushed long-term in-
> tegrity to the side, no matter what color you are or what class
> you are. . . . And we have to be honest [and] . . . tell the truth
> about it. That's the only way we're going to turn it around.
>
> —CORNEL WEST[1]

AFTER NEARLY FIFTY YEARS of helping to start scores of democratic public schools, I say with confidence that it is indeed possible to provide all children—the most and least privileged among
us—with an education that develops both individual interests and
an empowered sense of citizenship.

Public schools that prioritize democratic values don't all look
the same, any more than do schools designed for the wealthy. Some
offer Latin and some don't. Some have students call their teachers
by their first names and many are more formal. Some have richer
art programs while others pride themselves on the depth of their
science offerings or their vocational programs. Some emphasize

sports and others don't. But even given this diversity of priorities, the schools we are advocating for all share a basic precept—that is, they operate under the assumption that their students hold our nation's future in their hands. Behind the details, it is this understanding that is foundational to an education in service of democratic citizenship.

We are not claiming, however, that changes in schooling alone can produce equality without also making significant changes in other aspects of children's lives and the lives of their families and neighbors. But the twelve-plus years students spend in school surely influence individual and collective outcomes in many profound ways.

Establishing a school based on the belief that all students will be part of the ruling class is an important start. But democratic schools also tend to benefit when they are able to develop within certain conditions. Writing *In Schools We Trust*, in 2002, I laid out the following key conditions, which, I argued, were the bare essentials for cultivating a strong democratic learning environment.

1. Schools that work best are *small*. Within them, people are not anonymous and interchangeable. Students are well known to each other and the faculty, and their interests and talents are acknowledged and honored.
2. Schools that work best have the *autonomy* to develop a system and culture of self-governance. They accept being held accountable for their work because they are in charge of making major workplace decisions.
3. Schools that work best are places that families and staff would choose, if they could. They feel special to those who belong to them.
4. The students, families, and community are viewed with respect, and parents are seen as their children's important first educators and treated as such—consulted and included in the school community.[2]

There may be more conditions, but there can't be fewer. I have advocated for these conditions as a means to an end, not ends in themselves. They are what we owe all human beings. But the ends matter too. One of the central aims in scaling up small, autonomous, and respectful schools of choice is to transform a two-tiered system of education, with first- and second-class public schools, to one system of strong, vibrant centers of learning that serve democracy. We see these as community hubs serving the civic life of the neighborhood—places where young and old engage with each other, keep company with each other. But the reform waters in which we now swim have changed considerably from when my colleagues and I were starting schools in New York City throughout the 1970s and 1980s.

I still stand wholeheartedly by three of the four conditions—smallness, autonomy, and family inclusion. But the term "school choice" has taken a divisive and often destructive direction, and I now recommend its use with some significant caveats.

It is important to understand the reform context in which I originally proposed these essentials. Between the mid-1970s and the early days of the new millennium, there was growing acknowledgment—at least rhetorically—among enough practitioners, experts, public officials, and philanthropists that it was both desirable and feasible to provide children with intellectually stimulating and enriching learning environments. This was a shift that seemed to be gaining traction across the country for a good stretch of time.[3] This is not to say that schools were generally better in the 1970s. We had all the same problems we have today: segregation, unevenly funded schools depending on zip code, and so on. Further, the idea of choice was being lauded by free-market advocates, then as now. But the overall climate was not yet fully defined by free-market values. The idea that public schools could be turned into a commodity or that they would be best improved through competition was just not a widely held view. And, so, I ventured forth, drawing on my own strongly positive experience to take part in one of the country's first relatively large-scale school-choice experiments.

In New York City, which had made only a few isolated efforts at integration, before charter schools were even a blip on the school-reform radar, East Harlem's District 4 (in itself as large as many cities' entire school systems) showed what could be done if regular public schools were granted greater autonomy and encouraged to innovate and promote voluntary integration. I was lucky enough to be one of the first educators to receive an invitation from then district superintendent Anthony Alvarado to gather together my like-minded colleagues and start our dream school in the fall of 1974.

Alvarado's vision was to make accessible to all children the kind of choices in school culture, specialization, and size available to the nation's most privileged families. Since poor families could rarely move in order to get their choices, the choices had to come to them. Alvarado aimed to accomplish this by establishing not just a few alternative schools that might draw the neighborhood's most savvy parents but an entire district with enough small schools of choice to serve the entire community without eliminating the existing neighborhood schools. He hoped to entice experienced teachers to put into practice their ideas of what might make a better school. As an unexpected bonus, these schools soon attracted parents from other neighborhoods, including a substantial number of white families, thus creating a degree of integration in the otherwise segregated district.

By all accounts, District 4's experiment was an undisputed and well-documented success.[4] East Harlem was one of the city's poorest neighborhoods, and its schools were considered among the most troubled in the city. Its big, impersonal school buildings were under-enrolled; students who attended East Harlem schools had the lowest test scores in the city, and the local high school had the highest dropout rate. Instead of closing ailing schools, as has become the trend in most major school districts today, Alvarado proposed facility sharing, housing several small schools under one roof. Unlike many charters today that take up residency almost always in underresourced public schools, the new District 4 schools served the same children, had the same budgets, and were accountable to the same district as the traditional public schools. Within the first five years, Alvarado helped to start two dozen unique public schools whose newly energized and committed families, students, teachers, and administrators turned around the neighborhood's bad reputation. Within ten years, truancy rates plummeted and high school graduation rates soared to well above the city's average. And, for what it is worth, student test scores began to improve as well.[5]

The rejuvenation of the city's most troubled district was rooted in the bottom-up nature of the reforms. And the crucial spark that ignited the passions and dedication of so many educators was the open invitation to teachers: start your own dream schools. Alvarado had the authority and courage to extend such autonomy to all schools, including the long-established public schools that, regardless of their poor records, were nevertheless seen by many families as an integral part of the community. Some of the old-school principals took full advantage of their new freedom, while others chose to continue on as though nothing had changed. But the important fact is that families were able to choose from a pool of diverse, interesting schools within their own neighborhood, which created a district-wide climate in which a great many adults—parents and teachers—felt they had accomplished something meaningful and special. As Emily explains in the previous chapter, such a high level of buy-in from school staff—and from families—leads to a strong sense of accountability to meet each school's articulated vision and the expectations of an actively invested school community.

Each small school became an important center within the larger community. And while families were able to choose from among dozens of interesting settings, the goal of choice in District 4 was to create an overall sense of cohesion and support, not competition. Alvarado and his board aimed to generate a sense of community-wide pride in their collective efforts. Some schools became more popular with families than others, but we were able to visit one another's schools and learn from one another's practices with the general understanding that we supported our colleagues district-wide, not simply within our own schools.

How Alvarado gained the trust of District 4 principals and his school board is important to consider. It took courage on the part of all involved (something that we acknowledge may be hard to duplicate). In fact, the school leaders he chose to head District 4's schools probably did not trust Alvarado at first, but they learned to, as he proved again and again to be trustworthy. When important decisions needed to be made, such as when the 1975 New York City financial collapse hit just as Alvarado's tenure was getting under way, principals could see that he was there figuring out how to save what he could. Later, when faced with the waiting list of families hoping to send their children to CPE1, instead of ordering us to grow—a severe challenge that is too often foisted on small schools (as would later be the case for Central Park East secondary school and Mission Hill School), he trusted my colleagues and me to start two additional small elementary schools and eventually a junior and senior high school (CPESS) partially under the District 4 umbrella.

This is not to say that there weren't troubles: there were some incumbent principals who resented the newcomers, parents who weren't always happy with their choices, and suspicions that test score results might have been tampered with. But, overall, there was a sense that we were all part of something important that we cared about deeply. Alvarado expected us to be accountable to students and families, but he understood that when everyone buys into a strong school mission and is accountable to one another, it's easier to find solutions that work.

Over time, Central Park East elementary schools, as well as several other District 4 alternative schools, began to garner a lot of positive attention, not only from local stakeholders but from educators and reformers, some from the Right and some from the Left, who visited from all over the country and, eventually, the world. There was wide interest in the fact that investing schools with freedom to actualize their respective visions and to choose their own staff would create a school climate that radiated with the energy of professionals who wanted to be there. There seemed to be general acknowledgment and even excitement on the part of influential stakeholders that small, exciting, diverse learning communities characterized by respectful relationships and new approaches to curriculum and pedagogy benefited all children.

THE GOLDEN YEARS: SCALING UP SCHOOLING FOR DEMOCRACY

The years from 1983 to 1994 were characterized by incredible forward momentum, during which we began bringing to scale ideas incubated over a decade in District 4. Students and families who had attended CPE elementary school began requesting that we start a feeder school to serve students in grades seven through twelve. This coincided with two important events. First, in 1983, Anthony Alvarado left his position as District 4 superintendent and became the chancellor of the New York City public school system, which, for a short time anyhow, made the possibility of going citywide with District 4–type reforms seem entirely plausible, if not inevitable.[6] Second, this was the same year that I met scholar and educator Ted Sizer, whose book *Horace's Compromise* was about to come out. At that point, Ted already had an impressive resume, and the research he conducted on the nation's public schools laid the foundation for several seminal books on high school reform. The thoughtful critique Ted made in his books received positive reviews from across the political spectrum, an early sign that, despite (or perhaps because of?) the increasingly conservative politics of the Reagan era, progressive ideas were gaining traction among mainstream education reformers and stakeholders.

Horace's Compromise came out a year after *A Nation at Risk*, the first federal report issued by the then newly formed Department of Education, which caused a stir for its harsh assessment of the same school system. Though there was overlap between the two texts regarding the mediocrity of too many American schools, each offered markedly different visions for the way forward: the *Nation at Risk* report was premised on the inevitability of mistrust, calling for the tightening of screws in the existing system through accountability. Ted's book, by contrast, emphasized the need for creating conditions within schools themselves that would be more conducive to meaningful teaching and learning, and to new forms of shared accountability for meeting the needs of the school community.

Ted founded the Coalition of Essential Schools (CES) and drafted the Nine (later Ten) Principles (see the appendix) based on the ideas he outlined in his book—with its focus on knowing students well in order to teach well (among others). Addressing the need for schools to evaluate student learning, the Ten Principles included an insistence that assessment of competence and determination of credits and diploma credentials should be based on demonstrations, not standardized tests. Students in CES schools, if possible, earned a diploma by engaging in research on their own and in collaboration with peers, and defended their work before a committee (which Emily describes in chapter 6). When, in 1985, Central Park East Secondary School (CPESS) joined the fledging CES network, so did at least a half dozen sister alternative secondary schools and an equal number of district elementary and middle schools.

Alas, Alvarado's tenure as chancellor only lasted one year, but in that time, he was able to strengthen the Alternative School Division under the direction of Steve Phillips, who was critical in the development of the CES network.[7] Alvarado had both the know-how and the power to help us maneuver city and state regulations and requirements, and to eventually obtain a state waiver for us to open autonomous schools.

We were a bit concerned about referring to CPESS as an "alternative" school because we were interested in continuing to move our work into the "mainstream," but at the time there was no better plan. We knew that survival depended on garnering the approval of local and state officials, and we started the New York City Center for Collaborative Education (CCE) as a way to do important "lobbying" on behalf of our growing network of alternative schools. In 1985, CCE became not just a lobbying arm but the local support center connecting a network of about a dozen elementary, middle, and high schools.

This period marked a particularly tumultuous time for the New York City Board of Education. Seven different chancellors of education came and went from the end of Alvarado's term in 1984 to 1995, when I left the city. However, with every new chancellor who arrived, Ted and I—he with his Harvard and then Brown University credentials, and, eventually, me with my experience and reputation as a small-schools reformer—went together to greet each newcomer. Some chancellors were enthusiastic, some tolerant, a few grudgingly let us move ahead with our plans. But for almost a decade, we were able to proceed with our increasingly ambitious plans.

For a while, my progressive colleagues and I met with so few real obstacles to our plans to scale up that we began to all think bigger. For example, in 1987, just three years after starting CPESS, I became the first educator to receive a MacArthur "genius" award. The timing couldn't have been better. The attention I received helped our new high school get a strong start (one immediate impact was that a funding plan that the district had initially agreed and then reneged upon, was quickly reinstated). It helped spread the word in a positive way—especially in the media—about our ideas and the work of the coalition.

In 1993, after the first two classes of CPESS seniors graduated, I left my position as principal and joined with a group of trusted colleagues to take the next step in spreading our work.[8] We came up with a plan for both expanding the number of new small CES schools and demonstrating how one traditional big high school building could house many small, independently operated schools. We'd start with Manhattan, then take on the Bronx, and then Brooklyn and Queens. Julia Richman High School in mid-Manhattan was chosen as the first site. It was not a neighborhood school (located in an upscale area, the students traveled there from low-income neighborhoods around the city) and had a graduation rate of less than 35 percent and high absenteeism. The idea was to simultaneously close Richman and replace it with small CES-style schools. Still, some families initially protested the school's closure, an issue we addressed by convincing the city to buy or lease office space to hothouse the new small schools until all the students enrolled at Julia Richman had graduated. Once the building was available, a diversity of small schools and programs moved in: a music theater high school started by staff who stayed behind from the old Julia Richman campus; four other innovative high schools, including the now renowned Urban Academy high school, led by Ann Cook and Herb Mack; a K–8 school; a program for autistic students; an infant center; and a teacher center.

We did manage to open scores of other small, democratic schools in other boroughs but fell short of our original ambitions. Nevertheless, thanks in large part to Ann Cook's continuous leadership from the start, the Julia Richman Education Complex, as it's now called, continues to be an exemplary model of what is possible to achieve when educators are encouraged to invest their creative ideas and energy in the work of starting and leading their own small schools. As Steven Phillips, former head of the New York City Alternative High School Division, conveyed in a 2017 Facebook post, Julia Richman "became the prototype for school redesign in countless school districts across the nation."

Another breakthrough came in 1993, when the Annenberg Foundation offered CES (and a number of other organizations in other major cities) $50 million over five years. We proposed creating a pilot "district" that would be free of most city and state regulations and would operate based on our own innovative accountability plan—to be approved by a special commission of respected educators. Our aim: demonstrate the value of school/community-based self-governing schools, including showcasing some alternative systems of accountability. We hoped to prove that a district of fifty thousand students (which we planned to grow over the next five years) could operate with a high degree of autonomy. Columbia University's Teachers College and New York University agreed to document this small-schools experiment in collaboration with the New York Department of Education's own research division—all funded by Annenberg.

The Annenberg initiative, which became known as the Networks for School Renewal, aimed to become a model for New York City and, perhaps, the rest of the country. In addition to support from the Annenberg grant, we had the hard-earned buy-in from most of the relevant politicians and officials, including the mayor, the New York City chancellor, the New York City Board of Education, the state superintendent of schools, and above all, the American Federation of Teachers' local and national chapters. They all signed on to this ambitious experiment in creating greater autonomy in exchange for enhanced accountability in approximately 150 K–12 schools.

But enhanced accountability in this case did not mean more testing. In fact, all four partners to the plan (the Center for Collaborative Education, the Manhattan Institute, New Vision, and Association of Community Organizations for Reform Now) were folded into our agreement with the state to replace four of the five Regents Exams with a performance-based approach. When finished, we would have been serving a mere 5 percent of students in the nation's largest school system. Still, it felt like a huge victory—a promising experiment in democratic schooling that seemed to be on the verge of becoming a national model. After all, fifty thousand students was small for New York City but was the average size of entire school systems in many US cities.

What conditions supported the progress we made during that period of expansion? There was a shared view among a range of stakeholders, from the mayor to the chancellor, union leaders, educational policymakers, experts, and education professionals, that bottom-up reform made the most sense. At least rhetorically, most agreed that those closest to the action—school leaders and staff—should be making the important decisions that impacted the students with whom they worked or lived. The question was what kind of support from the top would make bottom-up reform feasible. Regarding the work that Ted and I, along with other like-minded educators, were doing, there was general acceptance of and even enthusiasm for the idea that the kinds of schools that the wealthy chose for their own children—schools that prepared people to rule themselves and their nation—were actually good for everyone. More than any one initiative, law, or source of support, the education-reform climate—again, in contrast to the general political climate—was simply more open to a broader conception of what it meant to be a successful school for all students.

Unfortunately, shortly after getting under way, the Annenberg initiative was cut short as Rudy Crew, a new chancellor, refused to support the expansion of autonomous schools. Even so, the co-alition work in New York City continued, and I still had reason to believe that our vision of school reform was a likely long-term winner. Of course, I was disappointed and angry that we were not able to see the Annenberg initiative through, and I decided to take a break from my direct involvement in New York City school re-form efforts. In 1994, I joined Ted Sizer as an urban fellow at the Annenberg Institute, where the Coalition of Essential Schools was housed. I missed the bustle of school life but wrote the book *The Power of Their Ideas* during that reprieve.

When we started Mission Hill School in 1997, as part of the then growing Boston Pilot School Network, I felt as if we were rid-ing an ascending wave, with Boston picking up on what we started in New York City. Perhaps unsurprisingly, when philanthropist

Bill Gates decided to set his foundation sights on education reform, he chose small schools as his cause, in large part, based on our CES-style work in New York City and Boston.

With the clarity of hindsight, it's now clear that we progressive educators underestimated how thoroughly our message would be co-opted, our vision of equal education distorted by a rising tide of market-oriented reforms. In part, it was a self-imposed naiveté, in part misunderstanding the signals that we were receiving. We didn't know that the vision of scaling up urban schools—proving grounds for democratic citizenship—would soon become severely marginalized at best and completely undermined at worst. We should also have been more concerned about the relative paucity of important Black and Latino leaders on our side and the general support articulated by major civil rights organizations for test-based reforms. Addressing educational inequity by closing the demographically determined test-score gap had soon become the myopic mission of the new reform era that emerged in and grew throughout the 1990s.

Nevertheless, I barreled ahead, focused on the children and families and colleagues in front of me. After nearly two decades of forward progress, I remained an optimist, determined not to be distracted from our mission to spread ideas that others could use to start democratic schools. Meanwhile, the nation's investment in democratic schools and other progressive alternatives was about to become buried beneath an avalanche of standards and accountability-driven reforms that threatened to end public education altogether.

THE BIG SHIFT: THE RISE OF MARKET-DRIVEN REFORM

The sharp turn toward market-driven reform brings into relief what democratic education is not, as well as the extent to which the ideas and language of one movement can be co-opted and distorted by another. As Cornel West's quote at the beginning of this chapter suggests, the only way we'll turn around the current corporate reforms is by critically examining the implications of their dominance and the damage done over decades of application.

Throughout my time in New York City, I spoke and wrote about our small-schools work and continued to advocate for school autonomy and choice. I argued that all three conditions—smallness, autonomy, and choice—must be considered *means* to creating a democratic culture within schools, rather than ends in themselves. Children who spend twelve-plus years in an authoritarian system—even a benign one—are not likely to understand the value or the necessity of democracy, much less how to be good citizens of one. For better or worse, my message resonated with educators and reformers from across the political spectrum. For example, in a 2000 analysis of the Annenberg initiative, one analyst from the conservative Fordham Institute praised the small-schools work I was engaged in, as well as my appointment to direct the initiative in New York City, explaining:

> [Meier's] selection by the Annenberg's agents . . . made sense in terms of what seemed like the most promising reform effort operating in the city at the time. [Though] Chancellor Fernandez [was] forced out of office . . . his legacy . . . was the creation of a large number of small, alternative schools, many of them inspired by or associated with Meier. By late 1993, this "small schools" movement was the approach that most national observers associated with education reform in New York City.[9]

I knew that we were walking a potentially dangerous line by using some of the same arguments being used by conservative reformers. For reasons I better appreciate today, many of my colleagues, including my mentor, Lillian Weber, were wary of diving into the fray of the mainstream school-reform arena rather than finding cracks that we could widen without having to risk the possibility of compromising our democratic aims. Though she was not happy about my decision to start CPE as a school of choice in East

Harlem, she nevertheless supported our efforts to make schools that serve democracy the national norm. That was our shared ultimate goal, and I found the support of wealthy foundations and mainstream, even conservative politicians irresistible in my effort to expand the reach of our work.

Indeed, there was a time when I didn't hesitate to accept help from large private donors. One of the best grants we ever received was from Exxon in the 1980s to pay for a longitudinal study of how CPE 1 graduates fared once leaving elementary school. As long as I thought it was clear that "we" had power over the work and its interpretation, I had no qualms about accepting their money. I think we did well by this standard. But I now see that even the spirit of educational philanthropy has shifted away from "charity" and toward dictating policy that shapes what professionals can and can't do in their own schools.

The ultrarich too often see themselves as the leaders and educators as the mere implementers of school reforms. This money-with-strings-attached kind of power is running too many publicly funded agendas; our tax relief for charity allows policy to be made by private interests versus public ones. Their aim: to demonstrate that education would work better, as would other public and private institutions, if they followed a free-market business model, with financial incentives in place, while starving out democratic voices and purposes. Schools that serve to educate a democracy increasingly seem like a luxury we can't afford. We are at a crossroads between these two ideas. The next decade will be crucial in deciding which path we will take in the remainder of the twenty-first century.

I guess, at least in part, that I have always hoped the fight itself was part of the democratic process. Yes, it was important to bring examples of progressive and democratic schooling into neighborhoods serving "those" (underprivileged) children, a job ignored by earlier progressive educators. Even if we didn't spread progressive education as far as we had wanted, at least the children we educated would be well served and would stand a chance of being better citizens with fierce concern for their individual self-interest and the common good. We hoped that CPE and coalition schools in general were living proof that this kind of education was as good for children who were rich or poor, white or Black.

But becoming the "norm" was unlikely to happen without the help of citizen activism, at a time (from the 1990s onward) when it has been largely absent, and without the support of our allies working toward greater equity in other related sectors, such as jobs, housing, and health care. In 1974, inequities were real but nowhere near those we face today, when the top 10 percent possesses 76 percent of the nation's wealth, and we expect that discrepancy to grow even more during the Trump administration's tenure.[10] From 1975 to 2017, inequalities became grotesque, while New Deal and Great Society era safety nets were gradually dismantled.

It is also with some unease that I now realize that I, along with some allies, in our attempts to support and foment citizen activism, actually played an active role in counseling individuals we now consider leaders of the "deform" movement. At that time, I think we believed there was an overlapping interest in figuring out how to redesign schools to meet the needs of a fully educated citizenry. For example, in 1991, a then unknown recent college graduate named Wendy Kopp sought out my advice about a new idea she had for starting what she was to call Teachers for America. As with the Peace Corps, the notion was to send well-educated Americans to bring knowledge to "backward" peoples. Only, instead of sending Americans abroad to spread "enlightenment," young Ivy League grads would be sent to the most underserved classrooms in poor communities across the United States. It struck me that Wendy had unrealistic hopes for what Ivy League graduates could accomplish from spending a few years in low-income schools. Above all, such schools needed well-prepared invested teachers.

A few years later, a young man named David Levin, cofounder of a then new small alternative public school program in Houston called the Knowledge Is Power Program (KIPP), visited Sy Fliegel, the former director of the Office of Alternative Schools for New York City's District 4 and a staunch ally of the CPE schools. Levin was seeking support to open a second KIPP program as an alternative public school in the Bronx, and Sy helped him do just that.[11] And, for several years, Bill Gates consulted with me and others concerning the progress of his foundation's small-school initiative. As we know, Teach for America, KIPP, and the Bill & Melinda Gates Foundation have become among the most powerful, recognizable, and well-endowed torchbearers of the new reform movement—a movement that, in conjunction with passage of the No Child Left Behind Act in 2001 and the Race to the Top legislation in 2009, has severely distorted a vision of educational equity that supports democratic aims.

The spread of KIPP and KIPP-style, segregated, no-excuses schools, for instance, signals our nation's shameful return to the pursuit of separate, and tacitly unequal, schools. On a surface level, Teach for America does civically engage college graduates, but it further undermines our social contract by sending the most inexperienced, young individuals into classrooms to serve our nation's most vulnerable children.

Regarding the role of philanthropy, while the 1 percent among us have for the past one hundred-and-some-odd years started tax-sheltered foundations and directed funds toward research, causes, and institutions they have sought to bolster, the turn of the new millennium has brought a significant shift in the way that philanthropists approach their relationship to education reform. Based in part on what conservative analysts have characterized as the lackluster national outcomes of the ambitious Annenberg Challenge,[12] a handful of billionaires have taken a more aggressive approach modeled on venture-capitalist sensibilities and strategies, using their fortunes to directly shape education policy.[13] In so doing, this handful of very rich families (primarily the Gates, Broad, and Walton trinity) circumvent input from both actual educators and the public, while the particular reforms they push—school choice, the high-stakes evaluation of teaching and learning, and *depersonalized* computer-based education, to name a few—also undermine democratic practices within schools and districts.

One factor that has made countering this movement toward market values more insidious and difficult to oppose is the cooptation of progressive ideas and open-education language. Ted Sizer's "personalized learning" once evoked "child-centered" classrooms, where teachers knew children well and students were able to develop their strengths and pursue their own interests. Now "personalization" refers to students moving through standardized instruction on a computer—no teachers or human relationships needed! And though Ted and other progressive reformers were once considered innovators, we are now accused by the new generation of reformers of standing in the way of progress and supporting the status quo. We have even stopped using the word "reform" ourselves because it has become almost synonymous with market-driven solutions to all that ails public education (and the world).

In fact, the very conditions that I have long argued are at the heart of school improvement have taken on meanings that are antithetical to the spirit in which I had always used them. The four key conditions—autonomy, small schools, family inclusion, and choice—which at the beginning of this chapter I argued were essential to recreating schools as proving grounds for democratic citizenship, have been thoroughly distorted by the current reform movement.

DISTORTING AUTONOMY

Autonomy is essential for allowing those closest to students (teachers, principals, parents) to exercise greater on-site power to put their collective wisdom into practice. We know from our successful experiments with New York's District 4 and the Alternative High Schools Division that it is possible for public schools within the system to use such autonomy well, as well as to use it badly. It depends on who possesses "autonomy." In this brave new world of reform, "school autonomy" has become a synonym not for self-governance but for more authority for principals or for the freedom of developers to control their franchises, with charter schools becoming the primary mechanism for transferring control from the public to private sector.

Chartering laws differ by state and, precisely because of their autonomy, not all charter schools can be lumped into one category. Many charters were originally progressive—often started by parents and teachers; in fact, Ted Sizer started a very good one in 1995 that is still thriving in Devens, Massachusetts. Many, many charters—the ones I call "mom and pop schools"—followed in this tradition and are run by my sisters and brothers in advancing democratic ideals and practices, but, alas, they now have virtually no voice or clout when it comes to influencing policy making.

Unfortunately, the money behind the charter (and now voucher) movements and the political aims involved soon became quite different: fairly early on, legislation opened the door to private entrepreneurs and chain-store schools that are the educational equivalents of a one-size-fits-all big box store. Though controlled by private boards, they are paid for by taxpayer funds. And though they only represent approximately 7 percent of all public schools, charters affect a much larger proportion of schools serving low-income communities by co-locating in their buildings and projecting a spirit of competition rather than community.[14]

Most of the charter chains and even some of the singleton "mom and pop" charters have been started with the support of rich business types who are opposed to the very idea that anything *public* is worthy of preservation. Some charters are frankly in the business of making money, and in states with lax regulations, it is often difficult to find out exactly what corners these school "leaders" (many of them with limited or no prior education experience) are cutting in order to turn taxpayer dollars into a profit at the expense of students and teachers.

The problem is that, in the current reform climate, charters have come under the spell of the all-mighty market concept. Instead of models of what could be done if all public schools had more autonomy, charters have been set up, in many instances, as an *alternative* to public schools to prove that they—by the very fact of being public—are inferior. At the same time, not surprisingly, charters could soon destroy teacher unions by disallowing their teachers from becoming members. Now, with billionaire school-privatization advocate Betsy DeVos as our secretary of education, we can assume that vouchers will come back into currency, along with their charter cousins, to threaten the continued existence of our public education system.

Meanwhile, many neighborhood schools in the most vulnerable communities are closed, and their teachers, disproportionately teachers of color, are let go, while parents scramble for other safe or even semi-safe havens. Often this precedes the gentrification of these neighborhoods. Public schools, at their best, are centers around which the community coheres. When they close, neighborhood cohesion in poor communities, at times tenuous, tends to collapse. It is on such cohesion that democracy's long-range future depends. Neighborhoods are where ordinary-citizen democracy rests. When it disappears, much goes with it, including a basic understanding of what democracy might or could be.

DISTORTING SMALL SCHOOLS

After Bill Gates began funding large-scale expansion of small schools across the country, the movement really picked up steam. Unfortunately, as often happens when the outward trappings of reform take precedence over the underlying function they were intended to support, they become hollow and, ultimately, unsuccessful. Scholar Michelle Fine captures the confusing moment of first "contact" between what would turn out to be two incompatible reform waves vying for defining rights to the same reform strategy:

> And then the winds of neoliberalism swept aggressively through urban America. In New York, in particular, philanthropy joined with mayoral control in a campaign to move small schools to scale. This was a heady and confusing time—was this good news or not? It soon became clear that the small schools movement was being co-opted and commoditized; Xeroxed and distributed across the city, with most of the key radical commitments of participation, equity, inquiry and dignity "left behind." Lifting only the numeric essence of small out from deep community moorings, the "move to scale" ripped the idea of small from the roots of participation, mistaking size as the point, rather than just a vehicle for justice.[15]

In New York City and Boston, we started small schools to facilitate the development of strong relationships across the school community as a foundational condition for fostering a self-sustaining democratic culture. Small school community allows every child and family to be known well by at least one adult at all times and allows the community to gather together in one space on a regular basis. Small schools make it possible to engage every staff member in discussion and decision making around important school matters. In short, small schools build a sense of community, support student learning through strong relationships with adults, and support the exercise of democratic practices across the school community.

On the other hand, small schools can adopt hidden agendas that are antithetical to the original goal. For example, they can institute a subtle way of tracking, as when gifted elementary programs become "small schools," thus entirely separating the children whose scores define them as gifted from all the "others." As for governance, small schools can make it easier for administrators with authoritarian tendencies to more closely monitor teachers, as smallness alone certainly doesn't guarantee that principals will share power or that trust will flourish. In other words, as with the issue of choice, small schools can be used to keep families, students, and teachers weaker instead of more powerful. Further, without a strong vision, small schools on their own may do little to address the problems that large schools contend with, while also failing to offer the benefits that large schools offer, such as larger social pools, sports teams, clubs, and a wider array of social options. In sum, divorced from a larger, more substantive goal, small schools can actually become the worst of both worlds.

DISTORTING CHOICE AND FAMILY INCLUSION

In the past, I pushed strongly for choice, mostly attempting to sway my skeptical progressive allies. I argued that it wasn't necessary to buy into the conservative rhetoric about the rigors of the marketplace and the inherent mediocrity of public institutions. By using choice judiciously, I argued, we could have the virtues of the marketplace without its worse vices; similarly, we could mine the best practices of private schools without undermining public education.

Counter to the push for free-market competition, I argued for choice as a democratic virtue. The ideal would be to make a wide range of interesting learning environments available to families within their very own neighborhoods, much like we did in District 4, where choice unleashed a wave of reforms as a means, not an end, for releasing the energies of educators with innovative ideas. This, of course, would require following the lead of District 4 in giving all public schools the same autonomy to innovate that, with a few exceptions, is a privilege enjoyed only at charter schools.

District 4, with its all low-income, almost entirely Latino and Black student population, also made a dent in the city's segregated system by attracting some middle-class families who were interested in the specialized programming and small-school settings. Unfortunately, this trend toward integration has reversed, with "choice" being used as a euphemism for offering very different options for poor families than those available to their privileged peers.

The mission statement of the American Federation for Children (AFC), a prominent school-choice advocacy foundation established and bankrolled by Secretary of Education Betsy DeVos, states that they strive to "empower parents, especially those in low-income families, to choose the education they determine is best for their children"; and in a recent statement, AFC president Kevin Chavous argued that allowing parents to choose their child's school "is the most democratic of ideas."[16] But conflating choice with meaningful parent empowerment and with democracy is a scam. Why? First, because in reality, marginalized parents are not the "choosers" under most choice plans—and least of all when it comes to vouchers. The schools, after all, can do the choosing, and unless we change the way most charter laws and private schools operate, they can not only decide who they admit but, in various ways, whom to expel and counsel out. Second, for poor families "choice" has become almost synonymous with the proliferation of no-excuses schools, environments defined by harsh disciplinary practices resembling the zero-tolerance policies that have so deeply scarred the very communities they serve. And, third, "choice" splits communities by creating competition for spaces and prestige in different schools and this undermining a community's political power.

Another common claim made among choice advocates is that competition will pressure district schools to "improve"—"If we can raise student test scores, why can't you?" the thinking goes. Another distortion made under current reforms is that *school improvement* can be boiled down to improving the test scores of poor Black and Latino children. This is, of course, an absurd proposition, given that public schools must take all comers, while charters can employ recruitment tactics designed to reach a selected audience. Fewer children with designated "special needs" or who are English-language learners are accepted into charters, and students with learning or behavioral difficulties who do get into charters leave them at a higher rate than they do with in-system schools. Ultimately, it is more accurate to say that competition works as a wedge that weakens the kind of social and political cohesion that communities (whether within schools or neighborhoods) need to help everyone build a better future for themselves and, importantly, for the common good.

My fear of choice writ large is that it will weaken the sense that *we're all in this together*—so essential to the fabric of a democratic society. Communal solidarity is too important a human characteristic for us to deliberately undermine it. We must feel invested in the overall well-being of our own and others' communities if we are to create a more just society. Communities that have fewer and fewer common institutions become limited in their clout. The needed solidarity disappears faster—and becomes harder to reawaken.

Family engagement involves much more than providing a menu of no-excuses and other segregated "second-class" schools from which to choose. Meaningful family inclusion necessitates that schools create a host of enabling structures: effective two-way channels of communication; clear processes for taking part in decisions affecting their children, which should include the right to appeal such decisions to an independent decision-making body; open forums in which to provide input and to vote on significant matters affecting the school community; and an open invitation to visit the school and classroom, as well as to get to know their child's teacher over time. The culture of individualism and competition that characterizes the current school-choice movement is not conducive to fostering any of these essential conditions in schools.

As many readers may have noted, there were many surface-level similarities between conditions that made District 4 a model for future reforms and many of the characteristics of the current reform movement. However, though District 4 may have influenced—or at least added fuel to—a broader, and what would turn out to be a divisive, school-choice movement, I also hope that readers recognize some essential differences. I cannot emphasize enough the importance of creating a system of choice that is rooted within each neighborhood, allowing families to choose a school without leaving the community if they don't want to. At the same time, it was important, for the sake of integration, to open schools to some interdistrict movement so that families could choose schools based on their offerings and not on location alone. At bottom, until neighborhoods are more integrated than they are today, we will need to examine the contexts that will allow us to balance building community with allowing for individual choices.

OUR ONCE AND FUTURE SCHOOLS

Deborah Meier

Not everything that is faced can be changed; but nothing
can be changed until it is faced.

—JAMES BALDWIN, from *I Am Not Your Negro*[1]

AFTER MY SHORT TIME working at Shoesmith in Chicago—that
small, collegially engaging, intellectually-vibrant-for-all public
school—I was hooked. I had gotten a taste of what it was possible
for public schools to be, and from that point on, I could not accept
that we would not at least aim to make our entire system of public
education as enriching as Shoesmith had been. That was in 1964,
and I have spent my entire career since working toward actualizing
that, perhaps naive, goal.

Even so, these days, it is hard to be as optimistic about the future of public education generally, let alone the possibility of significantly scaling up democratic schooling, as I had at one time
thought we might be ready to do. In the mid-1980s, for instance,
a more heady time for progressive educators, as I describe in the
previous chapter, my colleagues and I started the Center for Collaborative Education (CCE) as an advocacy and support organization that would facilitate the expansion of our network of small,
democratic schools across New York City. Later, in my proposal

to scale up that work even further as part of the 1993 Annenberg Challenge, we wrote, "The goal . . . is to bring present city school reform efforts to scale, creating a critical mass of small, effective schools, committed to equity, that serve the full range of New York City's children *so that the principles on which such schools are based are no longer considered 'alternative' but rather 'good practice'"* (emphasis added).[2]

Today, while there are still schools that have held true to their early innovations, managing to dodge mandates that would undermine their ability to meet the actual needs of their constituents, we are far from making such schools the norm. Instead, many of the democratic school projects that I was involved in over the past half century are in various states of peril or have already faded from existence: with New York City's District 4, once internationally recognized as a model of what was possible for a public school district to become, its garden of small, interesting schools has now all but dried up; two of the four Central Park East schools have closed and only one remains somewhat democratically governed; the original CPE 1—though it had a good thirty-year run—has been struggling for the past decade to hold on to its progressive practices and democratic spirit. What's more, conservative analysts have panned the Annenberg Challenge as a failure for its diffuse funding plan; the Coalition of Essential Schools held its last conference and closed its offices in 2016; and the very institution of public education is under attack as never before.

As of the publication of this book, a grossly unqualified billionaire president has appointed equally inexperienced, self-interested "one-percent-ers" to essentially dissolve the very public institutions they are entrusted to lead. True to this mission, secretary of education Betsy DeVos's 2018 education budget proposes to cut $10.6 billion from public education, eliminating twenty-two programs, including teacher training, after-school programming, and student-loan forgiveness programs (fittingly, she has appointed the

CEO of a student loan company to head the student loan agency). In addition, the secretary's budget would spend $1.4 billion to fund school choice, including a national voucher program.[3] While the rhetoric claims this is intended to "empower" poor families, research on existing voucher programs shows that such claims are based on free market ideology rather than on honest interest in improving the odds for those of us outside of the top 1 percent.[4]

Selling out our public schools in this manner effectively shreds the social contract upon which our democracy depends. As someone who has spent a lifetime struggling against the top-down and impersonal tendencies of our public bureaucracies, I am the first to acknowledge that there is much room for improvement! Nevertheless, it is important to keep in mind that the guiding principles underlying our public institutions—imperfect though they may be—are based on the assumption that we all share interest in a common good. The guiding principles of the free market are profit and individual self-interest.

Some proponents of the charter and, now, voucher movements truly believe that private-sector values and practices will address educational inequities by cutting through public school bureaucracy to provide poor students with more and better choices; others simply see school privatization as an opportunity to cash in on public dollars. In reality, the closing of our public schools is part of a larger trend toward allowing some cities and towns to become dystopian shells, vulnerable to crumbling or collapsed infrastructure and increasingly toxic living environments for those who have been left behind. At the same time, other cities are becoming unaffordable even for the middle class. As such, schools and their communities are falling prey to what we argue has become an increasingly "uncivil" society—one in which the freedom for a tiny elite to endlessly increase their advantage and wealth has overtaken our concern for the commonweal.

Corporate reformers have used the notion of *failure* as a cudgel to justify dismantling our public schools and turning everything into a business proposition. Educators who enter the profession because they are passionate about helping children are now held hostage to bottom lines, higher test scores, greater efficiency, and so forth to prove that they are not contributing to school failure. In all too many instances, however, the failure of public schools to meet the needs of their poor and minority students should rightly be attributed to a lack of human and material resources that schools serving wealthy communities provide, a problem that DeVos's proposed 2018 education budget would assuredly magnify.[5]

In addition, much of what in the current climate is considered "failure" might more accurately be defined as an inevitable stage in a longer process of change. As anyone who works in schools (or in any field, I suspect) will attest, we learn from our mistakes and, yes, from our failures. We make important decisions based at least as much, if not more, on what we find *doesn't* work as we do on what does. And what works well for one group or purpose today will inevitably "fail" at some point down the road as intentions, opinions, populations, and landscapes shift over time. In reality, there is rarely just one right or wrong answer or solution that will fully resolve the problems we face. And even when we do solve this or that issue with our schools, we know the problems are not fixed forever.

Responding wisely to flagging practices or systems requires those most knowledgeable and most impacted—those on the ground inside our schools—to take an "it depends" stance, to reflect on what has changed, what specifically has caused the breakdown, and then to use their collective judgment to decide how best to act. But it is not possible for practitioners to take such an open stance if they are forever on the defensive or if they are not given the time and space to get into the habit of reflecting on problems and how to work together to address them. For this to change, we need a paradigm shift away from paternalistic accountability and reform and toward seeing schools as unique communities animated by empowered constituents. As it is, external players have been setting what education scholar Anthony Bryk describes as "miracle" goals, disconnected from practitioner knowledge, scholarly research, and, most problematic, from reality. This has caused a "chasm" to open up between what practitioners are actually able to do and the constant declarations made by politicians and policymakers about the "miracles" that will be performed on their watch (e.g., that every child will have a proficient score on standardized tests by such and such a date, or that every child will successfully "race to the top" of some peak of ambiguous academic glory). As Bryk explains:

> We have thrown a rapidly increasing number of new ideas at our education systems over the past decade but often without the practical know-how and the necessary expertise to make these ideas really work. We overpromise and then get frustrated about how difficult the work is and how much time it takes to move from what seems like a good idea to effective execution at scale. We become disillusioned about the reform, it fades into the background, and then we just move on to the next new idea. Rarely do we stop to reflect. . . . Our causal postmortems tend to blame the individuals most immediately involved but fail to see how the task and organizational complexity that characteristics of contemporary educational systems shapes much of the consequences that emerge.[6]

In a more balanced vision of education reform, the role of external players—state and federal agencies, policymakers, and the like—should be one of support, providing resources, time, and space to work through the inevitable institutional inadequacies and shortcomings as they arise. And, of course, they should continue to create policies that protect vulnerable populations from discrimination and ensure equity and integration across school settings. Beyond that, the nitty-gritty of daily decisions should be left to the people who know their particular community and children best—families and educators. One of my heroes, Eugene Debs, once wrote, "I would not lead you to the promised land even if I could, for if I could lead there then others could lead you back again." When I was a young teacher, these words both intrigued and confused. Through my work with colleagues creating democratic communities, I came to understand his words—and to complete his phrase with my own: "we must lead ourselves."

For it is in working through the daily problems that educators faced with our students, families, and colleagues that we learned more about the dilemmas that a democracy inevitability runs into and how to get comfortable grappling with the system's inevitable flaws and trade-offs. And it is also through such grappling that we are able to model democratic practices and values for students, which is why I have always argued that teachers' formal and informal discussions should be held within students' earshot whenever possible. It is precisely those experiences with democratic life that most children (and adults) have never seen or been a part of. We cannot continue to let our young reach voting age without such real-life experiences. It is far too costly.

Despite all, I still stand by my words written over twenty years ago in the conclusion of *The Power of Their Ideas*: "No matter how bad things seem today or what bad news may come tomorrow, what makes me hopeful is our infinite capacity for inventing the future, imagining things otherwise."[7] Indeed, there are as many possible futures for our schools as we can imagine.

But not all the choices we make are conducive to advancing a democratic vision rooted in a sense of shared citizenship. Our commitment to democracy is being tested now more than ever. We have to decide if we are willing to forgo the opportunity to win the proverbial lottery that will propel us into the lucky 1 percent (which is the version of the American Dream that our current system offers) or whether to act as if everyone's kids were our own, as if our future prospects and those of our children brightened or dimmed in proportion to the prospects of others.

And so those of us who are invested in the idea of a common-weal—educators, families, scholars, activists—must continue to work to make our fragile democracy more robust, in our schools as on many other fronts. To think that we have failed at our quest for more equitable and democratic schools is to invalidate the work of those who work within the cracks, some as small as a single school, such as the Brooklyn New School, a public elementary that has developed its own performance assessments in place of standardized tests; a group of schools, such as those in the New York Performance Assessment Consortium going against the grain and thriving year after year, and many of the Boston Pilot Schools, including the Mission Hill School now entering its third decade; or as big as an entire state, such as New Hampshire, trail-blazing an accountability system that dares to put the horse before the cart by allowing values and research to guide practices and not the reverse.

The last "golden age" of progressive education reform that we were part of in New York and Boston, during which a variety of experiments in trust began to take root, happened not by accident and not just because of a few good administrators. It was made possible by an all too brief sea change in the national political conversation. At various periods in our history, there has been a public commitment to wage war on poverty and strive for racial equality. While most of President Johnson's Great Society programs ended much too soon and have been followed by decades of retreat, there's a restlessness abroad in the land right now that just might, *might* augur another sea change. And maybe this time we will be wiser and stick with a generous view of our fellow beings for the duration of our journey toward fulfilling the lofty democratic promise held in our nation's founding documents.

So, in our dreams for the future, public schools—regardless of how they are organized or the particular curriculum or pedagogy they adopt—will prioritize helping each successive generation, starting in early childhood, to internalize the idea that they are part of the "deciding class," as entitled as anyone else to make a mark on the world. To do that, we must first believe that the future has not yet been decided. Learning even this is a central role of schooling *for* democracy. Democratic schools help the future stewards of our society to develop essential habits of mind: to cultivate a healthy, informed skepticism in combination with a capacity for empathy that helps them step into the shoes of others and for playfulness that allows them to imagine how things might be otherwise. Finally, schooling for democracy guides children to discover and develop their individual passions and strengths, while also enhancing their sense of belonging and responsibility to the greater society.

I still advocate for smallness, autonomy, family inclusion, and, in some cases, with care, choice. But these conditions cannot be separated from the critical humanist principles that perhaps my colleagues and I took for granted when we started our schools based on these ideas. Something that has been too often trampled by the charter- and now voucher-led versions of the small-autonomous-choice reform movement is the connection we made between education for democracy and providing all students with the kind of intellectually vibrant education that has traditionally been reserved for the privileged.

As James Baldwin's quote at the beginning of this chapter suggests, we will have to face our historic and enduring demons—our entrenched legacy of classism and racism, among many other isms, as well as our national obsession with efficiency and quantification—if we hope to begin to truly wrestle with and perhaps even, someday, overcome those demons. Schools are, of course, just one of the important institutions that need to be rethought if "this

APPENDIX

MISSION HILL SCHOOL'S FIVE HABITS OF MIND

The Mission Hill Habits of Mind are an approach to both the traditional academic disciplines (math, science, literature, and history) and the interdisciplinary stuff of ordinary life. They are what lead us to ask good questions and seek solid answers. They are the school's definition of a well-educated person.

- EVIDENCE: *How do we know what's true and false? What evidence counts? How sure can we be? What makes it credible to us? This includes using the scientific method and more.*
- VIEWPOINT: *How else might this look like if we stepped into other shoes? If we were looking at it from a different direction? If we had a different history or expectation? This requires the exercise of informed "empathy" and imagination. It requires flexibility of mind.*
- CONNECTIONS/CAUSE AND EFFECT: *Is there a pattern? Have we seen something like this before? What are the possible consequences?*
- CONJECTURE: *Could it have been otherwise? Supposing that? What if…? This habit requires use of the imagination, as well as knowledge of alternative possibilities. It includes the habits described above.*
- RELEVANCE: *Does it matter? Who cares?*

None of these five habits stands separately, and the way we use such habits differs if we are studying a mathematical proof, a scientific hypothesis, a historical dispute, a debate over economics, the appreciation of a piece of art, a critique of a novel, the telling of a myth or narrative, or the settling of a playground dispute.

MISSION HILL SCHOOL'S FOUR HABITS OF WORK

- FORETHOUGHT: Thinking ahead and planning. *What will the work look like? How might this affect others? How will I complete this task with the resources available to me?*
- PERSEVERANCE: Sticking to the task, even when it is challenging. *When is my work due? What do I need to complete my task? What models, tools, or strategies will help me complete my work? Who will I work with?*
- PRODUCTION: Creating something that demonstrates what you know or have learned. *What can I create with my hands, my body, or my voice that shows my application or learning through practice of a skill or concept? What can I create with my hands, my body, or my voice that shows what I can accomplish? Who will I work with?*
- REFLECTION: Thinking about the work; pondering. *What did I learn? What skill did I practice or improve? What am I proud of? What will change about my work next time? What will I seek help in for improvement? Who will I ask for feedback?*

Both sets of "habits" are developed in the process of gathering appropriate knowledge and skill in school and out. The best test is whether students use such habits in the course of their work. And again, not just in school. Knowing "how-to" is no substitute for having good habits. Who cares if you could drive well, if you're not in the habit of doing so? Who cares if you could be on time, if you never are?

THE COALITION OF ESSENTIAL SCHOOLS' TEN PRINCIPLES

- *Learning to use one's mind well*
  - The school should focus on helping young people learn to use their minds well. Schools should not be "comprehensive" if such a claim is made at the expense of the school's central intellectual purpose.

- *Less is more: depth over coverage*
  - The school's goal should be simple: that each student master a limited number of essential skills and areas of knowledge. While these skills and areas will, to varying degrees, reflect the traditional academic disciplines, the program's design should be shaped by the intellectual and imaginative powers and competencies that the students need, rather than by "subjects" as conventionally defined. The aphorism "less is more" should dominate: curricular decisions should be guided by the aim of thorough student mastery and achievement rather than by an effort to merely cover content.

- *Goals apply to all students*
  - The school's goals should apply to all students, though the means to achieve these goals will vary as those students themselves vary. School practice should be tailor-made to meet the needs of every group or class of students.

- *Personalization*
  - Teaching and learning should be personalized to the maximum feasible extent. Efforts should be directed toward a goal that no teacher have direct responsibility for more than eighty students in the high school and middle school and no more than twenty in the elementary school. To capitalize on this personalization, decisions about the details of the course of study, the use of students' and

teachers' time and the choice of teaching materials and specific pedagogies must be unreservedly placed in the hands of the principal and staff.

- *Student-as-worker, teacher-as-coach*
  - The governing practical metaphor of the school should be "student-as-worker," rather than the more familiar metaphor of "teacher as deliverer of instructional services." Accordingly, a prominent pedagogy will be coaching students to learn how to learn and thus to teach themselves.

- *Demonstration of mastery*
  - Teaching and learning should be documented and assessed with tools based on student performance of real tasks. Students not yet at appropriate levels of competence should be provided intensive support and resources to assist them in quickly meeting standards. Multiple forms of evidence, ranging from ongoing observation of the learner to completion of specific projects, should be used to better understand the learner's strengths and needs, and to plan for further assistance. Students should have opportunities to exhibit their expertise before family and community. The diploma should be awarded upon a successful final demonstration of mastery for graduation: an "exhibition." As the diploma is awarded when earned, the school's program proceeds with no strict age grading and with no system of "credits earned" by "time spent" in class.

- *A tone of decency and trust*
  - The tone of the school should explicitly and self-consciously stress values of unanxious expectation, of trust, and of decency (fairness, generosity, and tolerance). Incentives appropriate to the school's particular students and teachers should be emphasized. Families should be key collaborators and vital members of the school community.

- *Commitment to the entire school*
  - The principal and teachers should perceive themselves as generalists first (teachers and scholars in general education) and specialists second (experts in but one particular discipline). Staff should expect multiple obligations (teacher-counselor-manager) and demonstrate a sense of commitment to the entire school.

- *Resources dedicated to teaching and learning*
  - Ultimate administrative and budget targets should include student loads that promote personalization, substantial time for collective planning by teachers, competitive salaries for staff, and an ultimate per-pupil cost not to exceed that at traditional schools by more than 10 percent. To accomplish this, administrative plans may have to show the phased reduction or elimination of some services now provided to students in many schools.

- *Democracy and equity*
  - The school should demonstrate nondiscriminatory and inclusive policies, practices, and pedagogies. It should model democratic practices that involve all who are directly affected by the school. The school should honor diversity and build on the strength of its communities, deliberately and explicitly challenging all forms of inequity.

THE CENTER FOR COLLABORATIVE EDUCATION'S FIVE PRINCIPLES

- *Competency-based learning*
  - Students move at their optimal pace and receive credit when they demonstrate mastery of competencies—or learning targets—at each new level.

- *Flexible learning*
  - Time, space, and teacher roles adapt to the needs of students through the use of technology and flexible structures, rather than being a fixed, "one size fits all" experience.

- *Student-driven learning*
  - Students exercise voice and choice in their learning and co-create personal academic profiles and learning plans focused on student interests, aspirations, and learning challenges.

- *Dispositions for learning*
  - With a focus on equity, identity, and concern for others, students develop the attitudes and habits necessary for academic growth and preparation for life in a global society.

- *Authentic learning*
  - Students engage in standards-aligned workplace-, project-, and community-based learning, with multiple opportunities to demonstrate what they know and are able to do.

SUMMARY OF LOS ANGELES UNIFIED SCHOOL DISTRICT SCHOOL QUALITY REVIEW RUBRIC CATEGORIES

- *Quality and delivery of instruction*
  - This includes educational equity and personalization; all students have access to, are included in, and receive support to succeed within a rich, well-rounded array of courses and activities.

- *Community engagement*
  - This includes involving families and community members in the life of the school and building a professional collaborative culture among staff.

- *Knowledge and understanding of autonomies*
  - This includes school initiative in the areas of staffing; curriculum, instruction, and assessment; budget; governance; and alignment of practices with the school's own pilot school plan.

- *Human and social capital*
  - This focus is on the knowledge, skills, and dispositions of the school's staff and "the intangible network of relationships that fosters unity and trust" within a school, as well as program coherence and use of resources.

ACKNOWLEDGMENTS

FIRST, THANK YOU to Andy Hrycyna, who planted the first seed in Deb's mind to write another book about her life's work. We'd also like to thank members of our Beacon editorial and production teams, Rachael Marks, Susan Lumenello, and Beth Collins, for your flexibility and patience in working with us through some of the obstacles life threw in our way during the process of finishing the book.

Many people helped us throughout the long process of writing this book, including first figuring out how we wanted to organize it. Thank you to those who attended our first brainstorming groups at the North Dakota Study Group in Brownsville, Texas, including Jay and Helen Featherstone, Krystal Akins, Rhoda Kanevsky, Lynn Streib, Rosellen Hoffman, and Yoshie Kittaka, among others. Similarly, thank you to everyone who attended our brainstorming session at the 2015 Coalition of Essential Schools Fall Forum in Portland, Maine. It was through our discussion that day that we came to think about this as an intergenerational dialogue, the idea that finally quickened (though not so quickly!) into an actual book.

We thank our friends who took the time to read early iterations of the manuscript and gave invaluable feedback, including Mike Rose, Marv Hoffman, Sonya Robbins Hoffmann, Yvonne Slosarsky, Melissa Kline, Rachel Henighan, and Roberta Logan.

To the founding Mission Hill School teachers: Heidi Lyne, Alicia Carol, Angel Alonso, and Geralyn Bywater; and to the

Central Park East Secondary School teachers: Marian Mogulescu, Mardi Tuminaro, and Pat Walter—thank you for helping to fill out our memories of our first thrilling years building these schools together.

Many, many friends and colleagues gave invaluable advice and helped us find needed materials, including Ayla Gavins, Dani Coleman, Larry Cuban, Mike Klonsky, Diane Ravitch, Monty Neill, Bob Schaffer, Sy Fliegel, Eric Nadelstern, Catlin Prestin, Margaret Blachly, Stephanie Lee, Ellen Schwartz, Joy Oslund, Shanti Elliott, Kate Keplinger, Lyn DeLorme, Eve Abrams, Ben McLeish, Nick Meier, Emma Rous, Christina Esguerra, David Berliner, and Audrey Beardsley, Pedro Noguera, and Ellen Pais.

We are especially grateful to Jane Andrias, who took over as principal of CPE 1 from 1995 to 2003, and who has been my stalwart ally and mentor in every project I've engaged in since the mid-1970s. Many thanks to Ayla Gavins, who has been principal of Mission Hill School since 2004. Thank you both for steering the ship with competence and grace.

Infinite thanks to our families who have been helpful in more ways than we can say. Deb would like to especially thank her brother, Paul Willen, for being "one of the only people who remembers what I did and said in my earliest years." Emily would like to thank her mother, Sylvia Gasoi; her husband, Winston Yu; and her daughter, Frankie Yu, for making everything possible.

Emily would like to thank all the families who helped out with child care so she could squeeze in many more hours of writing: Leann Trowbridge and Chris Lewis, Alison Brody and Ben Harbert, Rona Marech and Josh Shannon, Mia and Peter Hayes, Sonya Robbins Hoffmann and David Hoffmann, Clancy Broxton and Pablo Saelzer, and Lexi Diao and Graham Smith.

Finally, Deb would like to thank her oldest friends and mentors, those, such as Brenda Engel and Eleanor Duckworth, who continue to inspire her and the many others no longer with us, including Ann Spero, Lillian Weber, Vito Perrone, and Ted Sizer.

FOR FURTHER READING
AND VIEWING

EDUCATION AND DEMOCRACY

Barber, Benjamin. *A Passion for Democracy.* Princeton, NJ: Princeton University Press, 1998.

Chaltain, Sam. *American Schools: The Art of Creating a Democratic Learning Community.* Lanham, MD: Rowman & Littlefield Education, 2010.

Dewey, John. *Democracy and Education.* New York: MacMillan, 1916.

Goodlad, John. *The Public Purpose of Education and Schooling.* San Francisco: Jossey-Bass, 1997.

Levinson, Meira. *No Citizen Left Behind.* Cambridge, MA: Harvard University Press, 2012.

Meier, Deborah. *The Power of Their Ideas: Lessons for America from a Small School in Harlem.* Boston: Beacon Press, 1995.

Noddings, Nel. *Education and Democracy in the 21st Century.* New York: Teachers College Press, 2013.

Perrone, Vito. *Teacher with a Heart: Reflections on Leonard Covello and Community.* New York: Teachers College Press, 1998.

Rose, Mike. *Possible Lives: The Promise of Public Education in America.* New York: Penguin, 1995.

COMMERCIALIZATION OF EDUCATION, MISUSE OF DATA, AND SCHOOL CHOICE

Abrams E., Samuel. *Education and the Commercial Mindset.* Cambridge, MA: Harvard University Press, 2016.

Chubb, John E., and Terry M. Moe. *Politics, Markets & America's Schools.* Washington, DC: Chronicle Books, 1990.

Cucciara, Maia Bloomfield. *Marketing Schools, Marketing Cities: Who Wins and Who Loses When Schools Become Urban Amenities.* Chicago: University of Chicago Press, 2013.

Dingerson, Leigh, Barbara Miner, Bob Peterson, and Stephanie Walters. *Keeping the Promise: The Debate over Charter Schools.* Milwaukee: Rethinking Schools, 2008.

Hantzopoulos, Maria, and Alia R. Tyner-Mullings, eds. *Critical Small Schools: Beyond Privatization in New York City Urban Education Reform.* New York: Information Age Publishing, 2012.

Klonsky, Michael, and Susan Klonsky. *Small Schools: Public School Reform Meets the Ownership Society.* New York: Routledge, 2008.

Lowe, Robert, and Barbara Miner, *Selling Out Our Schools: Vouchers, Markets, and the Future of Public Education.* Milwaukee: Rethinking Schools, 1996.

Ravitch, Diane. *The Death and Life of the Great American School System: How Testing and Choice Are Undermining Education.* New York: Basic Books, 2010.

Schneider, Mercedes K. *School Choice: The End of Public Education?* New York: Teachers College Press, 2016.

TEACHING, LEARNING, AND PROGRESSIVE EDUCATION

Cuffaro, Harriet K. *Experimenting with the World: John Dewey and the Early Childhood Classroom.* New York, Teacher College Press, 1995.

Dewey, John. *Experience and Education.* New York: Touchstone, 1938.

Dinnerstein, Renee. *Choice Time: How to Deepen Learning Through Inquiry and Play, PreK–2.* Portsmouth, NH: Heinemann, 2016.

Duckworth, Eleanor. *The Having of Wonderful Ideas: And Other Essays on Teaching and Learning.* New York: Teacher College Press, 1987.

Engel, Brenda S., and Anne C. Martin, eds. *Holding Values: What We Mean by Progressive Education.* Portsmouth, NH: Heinemann, 2005.

Genishi, Celia, and Anne Haas Dyson. *Children, Language, and Literacy: Diverse Learners in Diverse Times.* New York: Teachers College Press, 2009.

Good Morning, Mission Hill: The Freedom to Teach, the Freedom to Learn. Documentary film, dirs. Amy and Tom Valens. 2014. Valens Productions.

Knoester, Matthew. *Democratic Education in Practice: Inside the Mission Hill School.* New York: Teachers College Press, 2012.

Little, Tom, and Katherine Ellison. *Loving Learning: How Progressive Education Can Save America's Schools*. New York: W. W. Norton & Company, 2015.

Meier, Deborah, Matthew Knoester, and Katherine Clunis D'Andrea. *Teaching in Themes: An Approach to Schoolwide Learning, Creating Community, and Differentiating Instruction*. New York: Teachers College Press, 2015.

Sizer, Theodore R. *Horace's Compromise: The Dilemma of the American High School*. Boston: Houghton Mifflin Company, 1984.

Weber, Lillian, and Beth Alerty. *Looking Back and Thinking Forward: Reexaminations of Teaching and Schooling*. New York: Teachers College Press, 1997.

A Year at Mission Hill, documentary, dirs. Amy and Tom Valens. 2013. Valens Productions.

REFORM, POLICY, AND SCHOOL CHANGE

Anderson, Gary L. *Advocacy Leadership: Toward a Post-Reform Agenda in Education*. New York: Routledge, 2009.

Barth, Roland S. *Improving Schools from Within: Teachers, Parents, and Principals Can Make the Difference*. San Francisco: Jossey-Bass, 1990.

Baum, Kenneth, and David Krulwich. *The Artisan Teaching Model for Instructional Leadership: Working Together to Transform Your School*. Alexandria, VA: ASCD, 2016.

Bryke, A., P. B. Sebring, E. Allensworth, S. Luppescu, and J. Q. Easton. *Organizing Schools for Improvement: Lessons from Chicago*. Chicago: University of Chicago Press, 2010.

Muncey, Donna E., and Patrick J. McQuillan. *Reform and Resistance in Schools and Classrooms: An Ethnographic View of the Coalition of Essential Schools*. New Haven, CT: Yale University Press, 1996.

Perrone, Vito. *A Letter to Teachers: Reflections on Schooling and the Art of Teaching*. San Francisco: Jossey-Bass, 1991.

Rothstein, Richard. *The Way We Were? The Myths and Realities of America's Student Achievement*. New York: Century Foundation Press, 1998.

Sarason, Seymour Bernard. *How Schools Might Be Governed and Why*. New York: Teachers College Press, 1997.

Toch, Thomas. *High Schools on a Human Scale: How Small Schools Can Transform American Education*. Boston: Beacon Press, 2003.

Tyack, David, and Larry Cuban. *Tinkering Toward Utopia: A Century of Public School Reform*. Cambridge, MA: Harvard University Press, 2001.

STANDARDS, TESTING, AND REDEFINING SUCCESS

Allen, D., ed. *Assessing Student Learning: From Grading to Understanding.* New York: Teachers College Press, 1998.

Boykin, A. Wade, and Pedro Noguera. *Creating the Opportunity to Learn: Moving from Research to Practice to Close the Achievement Gap.* Alexandria, VA: ASCD, 2011.

Carini, Patricia. *Starting Strong: A Different Look at Children, Schools, and Standards.* New York: Teachers College Press, 2001.

Carnoy, M., R. Elmore, and L. Siskin. *The New Accountability: High Schools and High-Stakes Testing.* New York: Routledge Falmer, 2003.

Chittenden, Edward A., Terry S. Salinger, and Ann M. Bussis. *Inquiry into Meaning: An Investigation of Learning to Read.* New York: Teachers College Press, 2001.

Darling-Hammond, Linda, and Frank Adamson. *Beyond the Bubble Test: How Performance Assessments Support 21st-Century Learning.* San Francisco: Jossey-Bass, 2014.

Darling-Hammond, L., J. Aness, and B. Falk. *Authentic Assessment in Action: Studies of Schools and Students at Work.* New York: Teachers College Press, 1995.

Engel, Susan. *The End of the Rainbow: How Education for Happiness (Not Money) Would Transform Our Schools.* New York: New Press, 2015.

Greene, Maxine. *Releasing the Imagination: Essays on Education, the Arts, and Social Change.* San Francisco: Jossey-Bass, 1995.

Hagopian, Jesse, ed. *More Than a Score: The New Uprising Against High-Stakes Testing.* Chicago: Haymarket Books, 2014.

Knoester, Matthew, and Deborah Meier. *Beyond Testing: 7 Assessments of Students and Schools More Effective than Standardized Tests.* New York: Teachers College Press, 2017.

Meier, Deborah. *In Schools We Trust: Creating Communities of Learning in an Era of Testing and Standardization.* Boston: Beacon Press, 2002.

Nathan, Linda F. *The Hardest Questions Aren't on the Test: Lessons from an Innovative Urban School.* Boston: Beacon Press, 2009.

Ravitch, Diane. *Reign of Error: The Hoax of the Privatization Movement and the Danger to America's Public Schools.* New York: Vintage Books, 2013.

Wood, George, and Deborah Meier. *Many Children Left Behind: How the No Child Left Behind Act Is Damaging Our Children and Our Schools.* Boston: Beacon Press, 2004.

RACE, CLASS, AND EQUITY

Alexander, Michelle. *The New Jim Crow: Mass Incarceration in the Age of Colorblindness*. New York: New Press, 2012.

Ayers, Bill, and Patricia Ford, eds. *City Kids, City Schools: More Reports from the Front Row*. New York: New Press, 2008.

Blackmon, Douglas. *Slavery by Another Name: The Re-Enslavement of Black Americans from the Civil War to World War II*. New York: Doubleday, 2008.

Emdin, Christopher. *For White Folks Who Teach in the Hood . . . and the Rest of Y'All Too: Reality Pedagogy and Urban Education*. Boston: Beacon Press, 2016.

Ferguson, Ann Arnett. *Bad Boys: Public Schools in the Making of Black Masculinity*. Ann Arbor: University of Michigan Press, 2000.

Kozol, Jonathan. *Savage Inequalities: Children in America's Schools*. New York: Harper Perennial, 1992.

Noguera, Pedro. *City Schools and the American Dream: Reclaiming the Promise of Public Education*. New York: Teachers College Press, 2015.

Perry, Theresa, Robert P. Moses, Ernesto Cortés Jr., Lisa Delpit, and Joan T. Wynne, eds. *Quality Education as a Constitutional Right: Creating a Grassroots Movement to Transform Public Schools*. Boston: Beacon Press, 2010.

Rose, Mike. *Lives on the Boundary: A Moving Account of the Struggles and Achievements of America's Educationally Underprepared*. New York: Penguin, 1989.

Rothstein, Richard. *The Color of Law: The Forgotten History of How Our Government Segregated America*. New York: W. W. Norton, 2017.

Stiglitz, Joseph, Amartya Sen, and Jean-Paul Fitoussi. *Mismeasuring Our Lives: Why GDP Doesn't Add Up*. New York: New Press, 2010.

NOTES

PREFACE

1. Arch Puddington and Tyler Roylance, *Freedom in the World 2017 Report: Populists and Autocrats; the Dual Threat to Global Democracy* (Dorchester, MA: Freedom House, 2017), 9.

2. Deborah Meier, *The Power of Their Ideas: Lessons for America from a Small School in Harlem* (Boston: Beacon Press, 1995), 4.

INTRODUCTION

1. See for example, Linda Darling-Hammond, Kim Austin, Suzanne Orcutt, and Jim Russo, "How People Learn: Introduction to Learning Theories, Episode 1, Introduction," *The Learning Classroom: Learning Into Practice, a Telecourse for Teacher Education and Professional Development*, Stanford University, 2001; Constance Kamii, "Direct Versus Indirect Teaching of Number Concepts for Ages 4 to 6: The Importance of Thinking," *Young Children* 69, no. 5 (2014): 72–77; John D. Bransford, Ann L. Brown, and Rodney R. Cocking, eds., *How People Learn: Brain, Mind, Experience, and School* (Washington, DC: National Academy Press, 2000); David Perkins, "Teaching for Understanding," *American Educator: The Professional Journal of the American Federation of Teachers* 17, no. 3 (Fall 1993): 8, 28–35.

2. See for example, Anthony Bryk, Louis M. Gomez, Alicia Grunow, and Paul G. LeMahieu, *How America's Schools Can Get Better at Getting Better* (Cambridge, MA: Harvard Education Press, 2015); Anthony Bryk and Barbara Schneider, *Trust in Schools: A Core Resource for Improvement* (New York: Russell Sage Foundation, 2002); Richard Elmore, *School Reform from the Inside Out: Policy, Practice, and Performance* (Cambridge, MA: Harvard Education Press, 2004); Michael Fullan and Joanne Quinn, *Coherence: The Right Drivers in Action for Schools, Districts, and Systems* (Thousand Oaks, CA: Corwin, 2015); Mona Mourshed, Chinezi Chijioke,

and Michael Barber, *How the World's Most Improved School Systems Keep Getting Better* (Washington, DC: McKinsey & Co., 2010).

3. David Arsen, Thomas A. DeLuca, Yongmei Ni, and Michael Bates, "Which Districts Get into Financial Trouble and Why: Michigan's Story," Working Paper #51, Education Policy Center, November 2015.

4. David Tyack and William Tobin, "Grammar of Schooling: Why Has It Been So Hard to Change?," *American Educational Research Journal* 31 (Autumn 1994): 453–79.

5. See, for example, Jane Anyon, "Social Class and School Knowledge," *Curriculum Inquiry* 11 (Spring 1981): 3–42; Michael Apple, *Ideology and Curriculum* (New York: Routledge Falmer, 2004); Pierre Bourdieu and Jean-Claude Passeron, *Reproduction in Education, Society, and Culture* (London: Sage, 1970); Samuel Bowles and Herbert Gintis, *Schooling in Capitalist America: Education Reform and the Contradictions of Economic Life* (New York: Basic Books, 1976); Annette Lareau, *Home Advantage: Social Class and Parental Intervention in Elementary Education* (Lanham, MD: Rowman & Littlefield, 2000).

6. Zora Neale Hurston, "Crazy for This Democracy," *Negro Digest* (1945).

7. Richard Clayton, "The Life of a Song: 'This Land Is Your Land,'" *Financial Times*, April 15, 2016.

8. Walt Whitman, *Democratic Vistas* (orig. pub. 1871; Iowa City: University of Iowa Press, 2010).

CHAPTER 1: THE PROBLEM AND PROMISE OF PUBLIC EDUCATION

1. John Dewey, "Education for Change," *Bulletin of the American Association of University Professors* 23, no. 6 (October 1937): 472–74.

2. Tyack and Tobin, "Grammar of Schooling," 453–79.

3. John Dewey, *Democracy and Education* (New York: MacMillan, 1916).

4. Erica Frankenberg, Genevieve Siegel-Hawley, and Jia Wang, *Choice Without Equity: Charter School Segregation and the Need for Civil Rights Standards* (Los Angeles: Civil Rights Project, 2010), 1–30; Simon Montlake, "Does Greater School Choice Lead to Less Segregation?," *Christian Science Monitor*, January 17, 2017.

5. My Mission Hill School colleague Beth Taylor wrote a weekly column based on children's conversations she overheard during recess, which, with our friend and colleague Brenda Engle, we later turned into a book, *Playing for Keeps*, about the importance of play.

6. Deborah and colleagues started Central Park East elementary school in 1974 as part of New York City's District 4 Alternative Schools experiment.

Between 1976 and 1984, she started two additional elementary schools and a secondary school, all in District 4.

7. Adler's Workingman's School was renamed Ethical Culture School in 1895. It expanded and became Ethical Culture Fieldston School (ECFS) in the 1920s. There are now four campuses: Ethical Culture, located on the Upper West Side of Manhattan, and Fieldston Lower, Fieldston Middle, and Fieldston Upper, all located in the Riverdale section of the Bronx. I attended ECFS for elementary through high school.

8. Progressive models such as Montessori, Reggio Emilia, and Waldorf schools were all founded with the intention of serving the children of working-class families. Today, these models are generally found in private school settings that few working-class families can afford.

9. The one caveat we gave students was that they would have to convince their families as well, and the debate of these rules was actually never fully resolved, with one member of the community or another raising it again and again over the years.

10. Harrison Jacobs, "The Revenge of the 'Oxy Electorate' Helped Fuel Trump's Election Upset," *Business Insider*, November 23, 2016; Jed Kolko, "Trump Was Stronger Where the Economy Is Weaker," *FiveThirtyEight*, November 10, 2016; Eduardo Porter, "Where Were Trump's Votes? Where the Jobs Weren't," *New York Times*, December 13, 2017.

11. Overall, a majority of low-income voters did not vote for Trump, but, as was true for Britain's Brexit voters, he won the vote of low-income and working-class whites living outside urban centers in economically depressed and culturally homogenous areas. It is also worth noting that self-interest and greed undoubtedly played a part in Trump's election, as a high proportion of Americans making more than two hundred thousand dollars a year also cast their vote for Trump. Finally, the clearest indicators associated with both Brexit and Trump voters were level of educational attainment and degree of cultural isolation. Skye Gould and Rebecca Harrington, "7 Charts Show Who Propelled Trump to Victory," *Business Insider*, November 10, 2016.

12. Rob Goodman, "What the King of Hawaii Can Teach Us About Trump: A Political Fable from 1819," *Politico*, January 4, 2017.

13. Rachel Aviv, "Wrong Answers: In an Era of High-Stakes Testing, a Struggling School Made a Shocking Choice," *New Yorker*, July 21, 2014.

14. Jason Nance, "Student Surveillance, Racial Inequalities, and Implicit Racial Bias," University of Florida Levin College of Law Research Paper Nos. 16–30 (2016): 1–79.

15. See, for example, R. R. Berger, "The 'Worst of Both Worlds': School Security and the Disappearing Fourth Amendment Rights of Students," *Criminal Justice Review* 28 (2003): 336–54; Randolph R. A. Bachman and B. L. Brown, "Predicting Perceptions of Fear at School and Going to and from School for African American and White Students: The Effects of School Security Measures," *Youth & Society* 43 (2011): 705–26; National Association of School Psychologists, "Research on School Security: The Impact of Security Measures on Students," 2013, 1–4; Pedro A. Noguera, "Preventing and Producing Violence: A Critical Analysis of Responses to School Violence," *Harvard Educational Review* 65 (1995): 189–214.

16. I use this term in reference to *Holding Values: What We Mean by Progressive Education*, a collection of essays edited by my colleagues Brenda Engel and Anne Martin (Portsmouth, NH: Heinemann, 2005).

17. Leib Sutcher, Linda Darling-Hammond, and Desiree Carver-Thomas, *A Coming Crisis in Teaching? The Teacher Supply, Demand, and Shortage in the U.S.* (Palo Alto, CA: Learning Policy Institute, September 15, 2016), 9.

18. Allie Bidwell, "Duncan Relaxes Testing Push, But Teachers Want More," *US News & World Report*, August 21, 2014.

CHAPTER 2: FALLING FOR DEMOCRACY

1. Paulo Freire, *Pedagogy of Indignation* (New York: Paradigm Press, 2004), 7.

2. People are often surprised that I remember anything from my nursery school days. My memories of what I learned at Head Start are actually surprisingly clear perhaps because of the stark contrast I experienced between a very nurturing nursery school experience and a rather traumatic kindergarten class taught by a teacher who didn't seem to like (or understand) children very much. See my essay on the topic in the book *Faces of Learning*, edited by Sam Chaltain.

3. Beginning the following school year, in 1998, and each year after that, MHS added another grade level up to grade eight.

4. Founded in 1994, the BPSN was intended, at least in part, to offset anticipated challenges, such as loss of teachers and students from the public school system, following the Massachusetts legislature passage of a state chartering law a year earlier.

5. Because MHS was housed in an old building that had originally been a high school, there was no playground equipment. The staff decided not to have a playground built but to keep the back area clear for "asphalt" games such as jump rope, hopscotch, tag, and football and keep a grassy area for imaginary play and exploration.

6. After winter break of our first year, we had a big scare when Deb became very sick with both encephalitis and meningitis. She was hospitalized and out of school for almost three months. Though we were terrified that she might not be able to come back at all, not having Deb at school forced us to take charge in a way that I think she was always urging us to do. In the end, Deb recovered fully and returned in the spring, and the three months during which we had proven to ourselves that we could co-govern the school proved to be very important to the staff's sense of confidence and shared leadership.

7. From the MHS mission statement.

8. Deborah Meier, "Democracy at Risk," *Teaching Social Responsibility* 66 (May 2009): 45–49.

CHAPTER 3: FALLING FOR PUBLIC EDUCATION

1. Friedrich Nietzsche, *Schopenhauer as Educator: Nietzsche's Third Untimely Meditation*, trans. Daniel Pellerin (Washington, DC: Regnery, 2004).

2. Perhaps the Trump administration's attacks on the bedrocks of New Deal–era entitlements and those that grew out of them, such as Social Security and Medicare, have led to a revival of attention to FDR's policies, as seventy-five years later, my daughter, Becky, is a leader in a Massachusetts organization called the Four Freedoms Coalition, which counters many of the current administration's policies.

3. In the mid-1960s, the Black Power movement began organizing into a political faction, demanding control of public institutions located in Black communities.

4. Though there were other small schools in Chicago, Shoesmith was nevertheless smaller than most, with fewer than four hundred students. It was also unusual for its high level of racial and socioeconomic diversity among the student body. Further, its diversity and proximity to the University of Chicago seemed to attract an unusual staff, most of whom were white women who lived in the community, had their children in the school, and who identified as activists.

CHAPTER 4: REINVIGORATING THE COMMONWEAL

1. Theodore R. Sizer, *Horace's School: Redesigning the American High School* (Boston: Houghton Mifflin, 1993).

2. Massachusetts Business Alliance for Education, *Every Child a Winner!* (1991), proposal for legislative action plan for systemic reform of Massachusetts's public primary and secondary education system.

3. Theodore R. Sizer, *Horace's Compromise: The Dilemma of the American High School* (New York: Mariner Press, 1984).

4. "Boston Protests MCAS Exam," FairTest, 2003, http://www.fairtest.org /boston-protests-mcas-exam, accessed February 5, 2017.

5. Title 1, in this context, indicates that a school serves a high proportion of low-income students.

CHAPTER 5: THE FALSE PROMISE OF HIGH-STAKES ACCOUNTABILITY

1. Nel Noddings, *Education and Democracy in the 21st Century* (New York: Teachers College Press, 2013), 3.

2. I later learned that I was labeled, in what were then "secret" cumulative records, as a "troublemaker" when I was simply advocating for my son. I can only imagine what names I might have earned in those cumulative files once I began advocating for the entire student body.

3. Deborah Meier, *Reading Failure and the Test* (New York: Workshop Center for Open Education, 1973).

4. Anya Kamenetz, *The Test: Why Our Schools Are Obsessed with Standardized Testing—But You Don't Have to Be* (New York: Public Affairs, 2015), 55.

5. See, for example, Linda Darling-Hammond, "Testing for, and Beyond, the Core," *Principal* (January 2014): 9–12; Stephen Jay Gould, *The Mismeasure of Man* (New York: W. W. Norton and Company, 1981); Jesse Hagopian, *More Than a Score: The New Uprising Against High-Stakes Testing* (Chicago: Haymarket Press, 2014); Banesh Hoffmann, *The Tyranny of Testing* (Mineola, NY: Dover Publications, 1967); Kamenetz, *The Test*; Alfie Kohn, *The Case Against Standardized Tests: Raising the Scores, Running the Schools* (North York, Ontario: Pearson Education Canada, 2000); Nicholas Lemann, *The Big Test: The Secret History of the American Meritocracy* (New York: Farrar, Straus & Giroux, 1999); Jay Rosner, "On White Preferences," *Nation*, April 14, 2003.

6. Roger Jones, "Robert Scott on 'Perversion' of Testing in Education," *Dallas News*, February 2, 2012, https://www.dallasnews.com/opinion/opinion/2012 /02/02/robert-scotts-t.

7. See, for example, Aviv, "Wrong Answers."

8. Ray Hart, Michael Casserly, Renata Uzzell, Moses Palacios, Amanda Corcoran, and Liz Spurgeon, *Student Testing in America's Great City Schools: An Inventory and Preliminary Analysis* (Washington, DC: Council for Great City Schools, October 2015).

9. In 1968, the city granted community control to schools in the Ocean Hill and Brownsville communities in response to complaints of neglect and

even malfeasance by white personnel within the schools. Read more in "The Tough Lessons of the 1968 Teacher Strikes," Dana Goldstein's article on the New York City teachers' strikes, published September 24, 2014, in the *Nation*.

10. The 1994 ESEA reauthorization removed the mandatory-testing provision for Title I schools and required instead testing all students with a standards-based (i.e., criterion-referenced) test in reading and math at least once each in grades three through five, six through nine, and ten through twelve. As Emily explains in chapter 4, Massachusetts led the charge, but soon all fifty states adopted what they called standards-based and supposedly criterion-referenced tests. This was the law until No Child Left Behind mandated testing in grades three through eight and in grade ten.

11. James R. Flynn, "The Mean IQ of Americans: Massive Gains 1932 to 1978," *Psychological Bulletin* 101, no. 2 (1984): 171–91.

12. Alan Vanneman, Linda Hamilton, and Janet Baldwin Anderson, *Achievement Gaps: How Black and White Students in Public Schools Perform in Mathematics and Reading on the National Assessment of Education Progress* (Washington, DC: National Center for Educational Statistics, July 2009).

13. Gould, *The Mismeasure of Man*.

14. Bob Shaeffer, *"Old" SAT Scores Drop Again* (Boston: National Center for Fair & Open Testing, September 27, 2016).

15. Rosner, "On White Preferences," 24.

16. Common Core (CC) Standards detail math and English language arts content that, it is claimed, every student should know by the end of each grade in order to be "career and college ready." The CC grew out of the 1990s standards movement, aimed at improving students' academic achievement through establishing consistent standards across states. Officially sponsored by the National Governors Association and the Council of Chief State School Officers, the initiative also garnered support from major philanthropies, such as the Gates Foundation, and the federal government, with the Obama administration incentivizing states' adoption of the CC by making it a criterion for obtaining funding under the competitive Race to the Top initiative. New standardized tests have been developed to align with the CC.

17. See, for example, Lawrence Delevinge, "Core Despite Controversy," CNBC, March 11, 2015, retrieved March 31, 2017.

18. Lauren Camera, "Assessing Assessments: The New Wave of Testing," *US News & World Report*, February 2016.

19. Steven Rasmussen, "Why the Smarter Balanced Common Core Math Test Is Fatally Flawed," *EdSurge News*, March 11, 2012.

20. Ibid.

21. Ibid.

22. Daniel J. Losen and Jonathan Gillespie, *Opportunities Suspended: The Disparate Impact of Disciplinary Expulsion from School* (Los Angeles: Civil Rights Project, August 2012).

23. Kristina Rizga, "Black Teachers Matter," *Mother Jones*, September/October 2016.

24. Campbell's Law, also known as Goodhart's Law, is actually a paraphrase developed after two individuals, social psychologist Donald Campbell and economist Charles Goodhart, who each articulated the law's premise in their respective works. In 1976, Campbell wrote, "The more any quantitative social indicator is used for social decision-making, the more subject it will be to corruption pressures and the more apt it will be to distort and corrupt the social processes it is intend to monitor." Donald T. Campbell, "Assessing the Impact of Planned Social Change," *Evaluation and Program Planning* 2 (1979): 85.

25. Dewey, *Democracy and Education*.

CHAPTER 6: MOVING BEYOND TESTS

1. Michelle Fine, *Educating for the 21st Century: Data Report on the New York Performance Standards Consortium* (New York: Performance Standards Consortium), http://performanceassessment.org/articles/DataReport_NY_PSC.pdf, accessed July 10, 2017.

2. MHS eliminated the "beyond the classroom" portfolio, so students now only need to complete five subject portfolios to graduate.

3. I only discuss a handful of formal assessments in this chapter, but the school also used several other formal and informal, school-developed and commercial or district assessments of student learning.

4. The Republican-led Congress passed a resolution in 2017 to annul federal oversight of state adherence to ESSA guidelines. Nevertheless, as of publication of this book, states are moving forward with their respective plans.

5. District of Columbia Consolidated State Plan Under the Every Student Succeeds Act, draft, US Department of Education, January 30, 2017, pp. 36–97.

6. Summary & Responses to Public Engagement Feedback on ESSA Consolidated Plan, District of Columbia Office of the State Superintendent of Education, March 14, 2017, p. 3.

7. For more information about innovative accountability initiatives, see Melissa Mellor and David Griffith, "Multimetric Accountability Systems: A Next-Generation Vision of Student Success," white paper, Association for Supervision and Curriculum Development, 2015.

8. Any LAUSD public school can apply to one of three autonomous networks: Expanded School Based Management (ESBMM), Local Initiative
Schools (LIS), and Pilot Models. Schools in all three networks are overseen
and supported by the LAUSD Office of School Choice.

9. The Boston Public Schools superintendent has discontinued the SQR process for Boston Pilot Schools.

10. The original CCE SQR rubric has been modified for use by the LAUSD pilot schools. See the appendix for a more detailed summary of the LAUSD
pilot SQR rubric categories.

11. A complete SQR review is conducted after the first three years for newly
established Pilot Schools and every five years thereafter or as recommended
by the SQR committee.

CHAPTER 7: WHAT HAPPENS TO DEMOCRATIC EDUCATION DEFERRED?

1. Cornel West, *Tavis Smiley Presents*, C-SPAN, January 17, 2013, https://www
.c-span.org/video/?c4322638/cornel-west-shameless-silence-progressives
-obama-education-reform.

2. Deborah Meier, *In Schools We Trust: Creating Communities of Learning in
an Era of Testing and Standardization* (Boston: Beacon Press, 2002).

3. Though the idea of educational equality has gained relatively widespread
support with the various civil rights acts passed in the 1960s and 1970s,
since then, the struggle for school integration has been more or less de-
railed. In the face of white resistance and even changing legal interpreta-
tions of the mandate, for good or bad, the focus for most education-equity
reformers has shifted back to the quality of the largely segregated schools
that serve predominantly poor and particularly Black and Brown students.

4. See, for example, David Bensmann, *Central Park East and Its Graduates:
Learning by Heart* (New York: Teachers College Press, 2000).

5. Seymour Fleigel and James MacGuire, *Miracle in East Harlem: The Fight for
Choice in Public Education* (New York: Random House, 1993).

6. In 2002, Joel Klein, then chancellor of the New York City schools, may
have come closest to doing so when he dissolved the power of local su-
perintendencies, replacing them with opt-in school networks and support
organizations. He, with the help of a former Coalition of Essential Schools
leader, Eric Nadelstern, used much of the same language as we had used
in our funding proposal to the Annenberg Foundation. But Klein was not
prepared to give schools more autonomy or to loosen the role of tests as
the primary form of accountability. He opened new small schools in the
old, large buildings, but most were top-down creations, not the inventions
of their faculties.

7. Alvarado was toppled by some irregularities he engaged in regarding the use of district funds, such as paying district employees for some personal services and allowing some employees to make what was considered excessive overtime pay; the charges were considered bogus by some and did not end his career, as he went on to become superintendent of New York City's District 2 just a few years after resigning as chancellor.

8. Ted Sizer; school leader and reformer Ann Cook; the alternative High School Division head, Steve Phillips; and the central head of citywide high schools, John Ferrandino.

9. Raymond Domanico, Carol Innerst, and Alexander Russo, *Can Philanthropy "Fix" Our Schools? Appraising Walter Annenberg's $500 Million Gift to Public Education* (Washington, DC: Thomas B. Fordham Foundation, April 2000), 6.

10. Jeanne Sahadi, "The Richest 10% Hold 76% of the Wealth," *CNN Money*, August 18, 2016, http://money.cnn.com/2016/08/18/pf/wealth-inequality/index.html.

11. The first two KIPP schools, which opened in Houston and the South Bronx, were alternative public schools, much like the District 4 schools. KIPP became a charter school franchise in 2000 with support from Doris and Donald Fisher, co-owners of the Gap.

12. See, for example, Sarah Reckhow, *Follow the Money: How Foundation Dollars Change Public School* (New York: Oxford University Press, 2013).

13. See, for example, Diane Ravitch, *The Death and Life of the Great American School System: How Testing and Choice Are Undermining Public Education* (New York: Basic Books, 2010), 195–222; ibid.

14. More than half (51 percent) of all students attending public schools are now reported to be living below the poverty line, as indicated by data on free and reduced lunch. *A New Majority: Low-Income Students Now a Majority in Nation's Public Schools* (Atlanta: Southern Education Foundation, January 2015), 1.

15. Michelle Fine, "Critical Small Schools—Windows on Educational Justice in a Neoliberal Blizzard," in *Critical Small Schools: Beyond Privatization in New York City Urban Education Reform*, ed. M. Hantzopoulos and A. R. Tyner-Mullins (Charlotte, NC: Information Age Publishing, 2015).

16. Kevin P. Chavous, "AFC Statement on Weingarten-Edelman Op-Ed," May 31, 2017, statement of the American Federation for Children foundation in response to *Los Angeles Times* op-ed from Randi Weingarten and Jonah Edelman.

CONCLUSION

1. *I Am Not Your Negro*, documentary film, dir. Raoul Peck, 2016, Velvet Film.
2. New York School Renewal Proposal to the Annenberg Foundation, 1993, p. 1.
3. Julie Depenbrock and Claudio Sanchez, "Here's What Betsy DeVos Said Wednesday on Capitol Hill," *nprED: How Learning Happens*, May 24, 2017.
4. Jonathan N. Mills and Patrick J. Wolf, "How Has the Louisiana Scholarship Program Affected Students: A Comprehensive Summary of Effects After Three Years," policy brief, Education Research Alliance, June 26, 2017, New Orleans; Patrick Wolf, Babette Gutmann, Michael Puma, Brian Kisida, Lou Rizzo, Nada Eissa, and Matthew Carr, *Evaluation of the DC Opportunity Scholarship Program* (Washington, DC: National Center for Education Evaluation and Regional Assistance, June 2010).
5. See, for example, David Mosenkis, *Systemic Racial Bias in Latest Pennsylvania School Funding* (Philadelphia: Power: Philadelphians to Organize, Witness and Empower, July 2016).
6. Anthony Bryk, "Miracle Goals and No Methods," in *Innovation in Odds-Beating Schools: Exemplars for Getting Better at Getting Better*, ed. Kristen Campbell Wilcox et al. (Lanham, MD: Rowman & Littlefield, 2017), vii.
7. Meier, *The Power of Their Ideas*, 184.